MAN THE

THE AUTOBIOGRAPHY OF
AUGUSTINE COURTAULD:
EXPLORER, NAVAL OFFICER, YACHTSMAN

The power of man is as his hopes.
In darkest night, the cocks are crowing.
With the sea roaring and the wind blowing;
Adventure. Man the ropes.

John Masefield

"All around it was utterly flat; in every direction snow stretched to the horizon like the sea. There was no life on the ice cap. I never saw a bird, or even a fly."

The Greenland ice cap station as the rescue party found it on 5th May 1931. The snow had obliterated all distinguishing features. Courtauld, who had been there since December, was trapped underneath.

MAN THE ROPES

THE AUTOBIOGRAPHY OF
AUGUSTINE COURTAULD:
EXPLORER, NAVAL OFFICER, YACHTSMAN

Augustine Courtauld

In memory of Augustine Courtauld: explorer, naval officer, yachtsman.

First published in 1957 by Hodder & Stoughton Ltd

Second revised edition published in 2021 by Golden Duck (UK) Ltd
Sokens, Green Street, Pleshey, nr Chelmsford, Essex, CM3 1HT
golden-duck.co.uk

Front cover:
Susie Hamilton, *August* (detail), 1998, oil on board, 37x42 cm.
Courtesy of Paul Stolper Gallery, London.

A CIP catalogue record for this book is available from the British Library.

ISBN 978-1-899262-46-5

Printed and bound in the UK by Biddles Books Ltd
biddles.co.uk

Contents

Introduction to the Second Edition [·]

RIEL'S SONG "Full fathom five thy father lies" used to haunt me in my schooldays because of its uncanny lyrics and because, in the case of August's six children, it was true. Our father was buried at sea in 1959. I was eight when he died and, since he was ill for several years before that, my memories of him are almost non-existent. One anecdote that I like, but don't remember, concerns my childhood fear of changes in appearance. I would scream at the sight of people in hats and when a woman came to tea in one, August, with characteristic suddenness, pulled it off her head and off came her wig with it, leaving her bald.

Although I have few memories, his personality and reputation have shadowed my life, influencing my paintings of figures (including polar explorers) struggling in wilderness. There is a beautiful entry in his diary about Arctic sun "casting its rose-pink light along the snow and making shadows" that found its way into "August", my picture on the cover of this book. He has always seemed to me to be a fiery, daimonic figure, a frightening but exciting wild-man who, though able to obey the conventions of society, in drawing rooms and committees, at dances and the Stock Exchange, really belonged out there in the sublime places of nature: the deserts, ice-fields, glaciers, oceans, mountains, fjords and rivers containing hippos and crocodiles. Maybe this is to romanticise or even dehumanise him but I am reminded of August when reading D. H. Lawrence's essay on Herman Melville: "the man who came from the sea to live among men can stand it no longer. He hears the horror of the cracked church bell, and goes back down to the shore, back to the ocean again, home, into the salt water." August was in some essential way an outsider and I always liked this quality, one that comes across forcefully in this autobiography.

I have often returned to *Man the Ropes* and appreciate its extraordinary account of courage and deliverance. As someone who is afraid of sailing (how my father would have despised my sea-nerves) his account of the storm in chapter 14, "*Duet*", fills me with horror. It is indeed like something from Melville, from *Moby Dick* perhaps. I am also aware of the miracle of existing at all since he came so close to dying in his ice-prison in Greenland. I am amazed by the extraordinary, eleventh-hour rescue just when "the Primus gave its last gasp" and am in awe of his religious faith that, despite all appearances, he would be saved.

The prose style of the book appeals to me. As his anthology of polar writing, *From the Ends of the Earth* shows, he was scholarly and well-read. He loved literature, reading the Brontës, Walter Scott, Pepys, Thackeray and Galsworthy when incarcerated on the ice cap, and he was an impressive writer himself. His spare, economical, quick-fire sentences even remind me a little of laconic prose masters like Orwell, Camus or Hemingway. They seem to express his wry sense of humour, his modest, self-deprecating personality—his hatred of "fuss"—and also correspond to the austere content of his book, the stark, barren landscapes he sought:

"All around it was utterly flat; in every direction snow stretched to the horizon like the sea. There was no life on the ice cap. I never saw a bird, or even a fly."

Susie Hamilton

Susie Hamilton is a British artist whose work has been purchased by private and public collections including the Science Museum and British Museum. She is known for her iconoclastic approach to painting, for her interest in metamorphosis and for depicting solitary figures. Since 2018 she has worked with the charity Hospital Rooms painting murals in mental health units.

Editor's Note

WHEN I first read *Man the Ropes* I didn't know quite how to respond. I had begun with prejudice, ready to dislike Courtauld for his social status and likely attitudes, for being so rich, for not having to work, for his ability to indulge himself materially. These were the circumstances of his life and there are certainly episodes in the memoir that may shock the twenty-first century reader. Others made me laugh aloud. Courtauld has a quality of straightforwardness which takes the sting from some of his more outrageous statements. He explains his failure to talk to his partner at a Cambridge May Ball: "In fact I had no use for girls at this time and thought them a nuisance." Later, while waiting for a command in the early years of WW2, he remembers remarking that "the trouble with the Navy was that officers no longer sank with their ships". "This didn't contribute to my popularity," he added.

He seems to accept the person he is, then carries on from there. His description of himself and his sister Betty as "those awful Courtauld children" sets the characteristic tone of honesty. People who loved him and were close to him often described him as "eccentric". Writing in *The Sunday Times*, Ian Fleming, who knew him both during and after the war, describes him as quixotic and prone to getting into "scrapes" with authority. Reading between the lines I began to wonder what labels we might stick onto him today.

The narrative tone in *Man the Ropes* is distinctive. Here is a terminally ill man telling his tale with no time to waste and nothing to prove. His wife, Mollie, is said to have disliked the book; others to have been "disappointed" by it. Yet Courtauld's biographer, Nicholas Wollaston, author of *The Man on the Ice Cap* (published by Constable, 1980) concludes that "there was more of the man himself in it than in many more ponderous autobiographies". Perhaps some of its unique quality does come from the simplification of severe illness; more may derive from the fact that it was told rather than written. In his dedication to the first edition Courtauld singled out his nurse, Sister Janie Howells, for "special gratitude": "Janie is not a secretary, nor ever will be. Her job is looking after me—quite enough for anyone. Yet she has written out the whole of this book in longhand. Without her I could never have done it."

Nicholas Wollaston captures the unique quality of this book when he says that the reader "hears" Courtauld "talking quietly from his bed about the things he liked to think about; no heroics, no grand attitudes, no sententious afterthoughts". It would, however, be supremely mistaken to approach *Man the Ropes* with an attitude of pity. Courtauld's life was one of strenuous effort, impressive achievement and an ethic of service. He was loyal and loving. One of his most frequently used phrases is "my old friend"; his characteristic adjectives are "fine" and "splendid" yet, also, as his daughter Susie points out, his observation of the natural world has an artistic sensitivity and unobtrusive refinement.

All the family members contacted have shown their enduring affection in their quick generous responses. It's especially glorious that *Duet*, who Mollie described as "a member of the family" is now the UK's longest-serving sail-training vessel taking less materially fortunate young people to sea. We are proud to include *Man the Ropes* on the Golden Duck list and offer our special gratitude to Julien Courtauld as well as to Susie Hamilton, Perina Braybrooke, Stephen, Elizabeth and Sarah Courtauld and Leonie Back from the Cirdan Trust.

Julia Jones

Foreword to the First Edition

I T HAS been a characteristic of August Courtauld that although he could always see with remarkable clearness how to steer through a storm, he puts the glass to a blind eye as far as difficulties are concerned. No doubt that is one reason why his life has been so full of varied adventures. But when he comes to dictate the story from his chair by the fireside, he makes everything appear so straightforward and simple that those who do not know him might think it really was. By giving another point of view—on two or three incidents in which I, and the companion to whom the book is dedicated, were personally involved, this foreword may make it easier for the imaginative to read between the lines.

Most people who are old enough will remember the headlines in 1931 about Courtauld "Lost on an Ice Cap". He at that time, nine thousand feet up on a lifeless plateau, in a tent buried under the snow, was of course entirely ignorant about what was happening in the outside world. I don't think he has ever fully understood what all the fuss was about. He had travelled in from the coast with a party which was to stock the weather station adequately for two men to stay there. Atrocious weather had so slowed down the journey that most of the food intended for the Station was eaten on the way there. It looked as if the place would have to be closed down and the series of observations broken.

"I worked out," Courtauld writes, "that [...] I could last out alone for five months. As I had frostbite in my toes, I had no wish to make the journey back. So I decided to stay on my own and keep the Station going."

A touch of frostbite is an original reason for choosing a winter of solitary confinement in a place where anything might happen since no one had ever seen it at that season before.

Unfortunately he says very little of how, mentally, he spent his time. He read while the books and fuel lasted. He designed a yacht. His pipe was a talisman, for it had been given to him at home. He sang songs for their association. "It was an awful row but there was no one to hear it." And he came to trust implicitly in God.

He talks of the stillness. "The only thing you could hear was the blood pounding in your ears." When three of us were trying to reach the station at the time of equinoxial gales we found that it was all too seldom still. When we were only a few miles distant it blew a continuous blizzard for six days and nights. One might as well have tried to walk up a waterfall as against the drifting snow. Inside the tent it was like suffering a bombardment. It tried the nerves of three men together. On one man alone and by that time in the dark, it seemed to have no ill effect at all.

That is only one incident from several Arctic expeditions. And he has explored sand deserts too. Lord Rennell writes of the journey which they made together.

"He came with me to the Sahara in 1927, having not many months before been on an expedition to Greenland. The contrast in life and temperature in a Saharan summer perturbed him not at all, and he contributed so much more than he describes that it would take more than a foreword to record or correct the understatements in his chapter on this journey. Apart from a major part in the survey done, climbing every hill or mountain in sight, keeping the pot filled wherever there was any game, he kept everyone amused and devoted to himself by his unending fund of incongruities and idiosyncrasies. He was no linguist, but made himself understood. His name for people and places required a glossary: an example is his obscure reference to 'Higher the Fewer', an incompetent guide on a fearsome 300-mile stretch of desert, whose real name was Khayar.

"Soon after his return, after nearly a year's absence in North Africa, Courtauld again visited his beloved Arctic."

Courtauld has had many adventures of a different sort fearlessly and obstinately crusading for the good of his fellow men. But I know he would not want one to enlarge upon that side of things.

For relaxation throughout his married life there has been the dream yacht of the Ice Cap Station, now crewed by his children. *Duet* has never been allowed to remain long at her anchorage—at any anchorage for that matter—when sailing was in any way possible. A certain club, where in his opinion too much yachting was done in the bar, once asked him if he would present a cup. He replied he would willingly do so—for the yacht which sailed farthest from the club house during the season, irrespective of other merit.

Duet has sailed far, and taken some hard knocks... But it is time to give way and let the Skipper tell his yarn of land and sea and people in his own manner—sometimes having a dig at things he does not approve of, but for the most part quietly and undramatically.

J. M. Scott

James Maurice Scott was a fellow member of the 1930-1931 British Arctic Air Route Expedition to Greenland. He had made several abortive attempts to find and relieve Courtauld before Gino Watkins, Freddy Spencer Chapman and John Rymill were finally successful in May. Scott later wrote Gino Watkins' biography.

The 'companion' he mentions is Francis Rodd, later Lord Rennell, to whom August Courtauld dedicated the first edition of Man the Ropes.

Author's Preface

I AM JUST an ordinary chap and belong to a family which my father used to say was "a very humdrum lot, very humdrum". There is no reason why I should write a book—I have always felt there were too many—but some of my friends have persuaded me.

I expect I shall be thought to be shooting a line writing an "I" book, but I only hope some of it may interest you. Anyhow, here goes.

August Courtauld
February 1956

Duet, *everything set.*

I

Little Bradfords

I WAS BORN at Little Bradfords in the small town of Bocking, Essex, in August 1904. My father had been born in the great vintage year of 1865, in company with King George V and Rudyard Kipling; my mother, about ten years younger, was a Maid of Kent, of the family of Lister. She was one of the few who managed to penetrate my grandfather's house at Gosfield.

As children we saw little of our parents. My sister Betty (two years my junior) and I were allowed to come down to lunch, and again at five o'clock for exactly an hour. On Sundays I used to walk with my father to church, a distance of about two miles. Generally we discussed model steam-engines, a subject of absorbing interest to me at that time. The rest of our lives was chiefly spent in the nursery, or out for endless walks. Now and then we were taken out in the pony trap, and when I got too impossible, I was set down in the road and had to run behind. We were awful children. There was the time I covered Betty's hair with plasticine to turn her into a monk, and then when I could not get the plasticine off, took her hair off too, with scissors. There was also the time when the neighbours opposite were astonished by the sight of Betty being lowered out of an upper window. I had been given a crane for a birthday present and was trying it out.

Discipline was maintained by Nurse (there were no kind nannies in those days). The gardener used to cut canes for her, and when these had no effect she would lock us up in cupboards. I well remember watching the carpenter mend a cupboard door I had kicked down. My father was usually immersed in a book and quite oblivious of what was going on around him. On one occasion I was playing with the curtain cords in the library and brought down a large bust which smashed to fragments at my feet. My father took no notice whatever.

We had two forms of entertainment. One was Morris dancing on the lawn, the other the visits of the organ grinder. He used to play in the drive outside the nursery window, and generally he had a monkey sitting on top of his barrel-organ. Once he brought a bear, and, as Betty had meanwhile disappeared, it was thought the bear had got her.

Our great treat was being taken out in the car, an open Argyll which clucked like a hen. Motoring was a bit of an adventure. There was always the hazard of getting the car up a hill in top: it wasn't done to change gear. And there was the great occasion when my parents bought a house at Frinton and we set out for it in the car. All the pets had to come. There was Breeks the Persian cat, the canary, and Torty the tortoise. We hadn't gone a hundred yards before Breeks escaped. When he had been recaptured, it was discovered that Torty had disappeared. No one was allowed to speak to my father when he was driving. I remember saying once, when I was sitting beside him, "Isn't it a lovely sunset, Daddy?" Instantly there came from my mother in the back, "Don't talk. *Daddy's driving.*" If there was fog, my father considered that the proper thing to do was to walk in front while his man, Howard, took over the wheel. My father's driving always made my mother nervous and after a bit he gave it up. It was said he had gone into the ditch one day when he was out alone. Usually he only went out in the car with my mother; otherwise he walked everywhere.

After a while we left "Cruel Nurse" and were turned over to a succession of governesses. The only two who stayed the course for any length of time were Bennie (Miss Bendall) and Miss O'Reilly. We loved both these ladies dearly. They lasted far into our school days and we have kept up with them ever since: Bennie until she died, while Miss O'Reilly was still teaching up to a few months ago, after more than fifty years.

Enemy Number one in those days was The Visitors. Children were supposed to be "seen and not heard"; our motto was "quickly and quietly". From the cover of the bushes, we attacked with bows and arrows. Produced for inspection, we would spit and stamp on the hats of the enemy. It is not surprising we were known as "those awful Courtauld children".

August, Betty and Peter Courtauld.
Amateur theatricals at Little Bradfords.

2

School

A T THE age of nine I was packed off to school in Eastbourne. My companion on the train was a boy called Heath. Like me, he had a bowler hat rammed down over his eyes; so far as I remember, we never spoke to one another the whole way.

St. Christopher's was run by the Reverend L. R. Browne, a kindly, fat, quick little man. He used to take us for runs on Beachy Head, and the older boys went bathing at Holy Well before breakfast when they had learnt to swim. Browne used to come and wake us by a touch on the forehead; after that it was a race on our bikes all the way down to the cove. How the sea sparkled in the morning light!

When we did badly, old Browne issued us with a yellow card called a "satisfecit". If we didn't succeed in giving that satisfaction, we were summoned to the Headmaster's study at ten to nine and there he beat us—when we were younger, with a slipper, later with a birch on the bare behind.

Coming home one year for the summer holidays, I found there was a bit of a flap on. My mother said there might be a war (at first I thought she meant another of those squabbles in the Balkans). We all waited in a panic to see what the Government would do and prayed that they wouldn't let Belgium down.

The first exciting thing that happened was the arrival of soldiers at Bocking. Down the road, past our house, came the column of marching men, band playing, officers on horseback. I rushed to the gate to watch them, fell down on the gravel and cut my knee, but was much too thrilled to take any notice of that or tear myself away from the wonderful sight of the marching men in khaki. People were throwing them food, rushing out with cups of tea. Later, the General (Brigadier-General Shipley) and his staff came to live with us. General Shipley's son also came. The General was an iron-grey man as hard as nails; his troops were the Sherwood Foresters, who came to dig trenches and defend us against the invasion. It was all tremendously thrilling, especially for the maids, who had the batmen living in the house. For many years afterwards, the maids used to hang up their caps at Christmastime.

Pepper, the General's batman, took young Shipley and I out riding on our ponies. Once, the General took us on a route march, riding one on each side of him at the head of the troops, with the band playing behind us. I remember, too, how he read us, in his deep voice, "The Drums of the Fore and Aft" by Kipling. My own favourite book then and for many years was Meade Falkner's *Moonfleet*, and I still think Falkner would have become one of our best authors if he had not gone into business instead.

Outside the library was a telephone attached to the wall. This was considered to be an instrument for emergencies and was never used. One day, however, an officer on the General's staff, Colonel Synott, thought he would try to ring up his family in Gloucestershire. He got through and actually heard what they were saying. This was thought a marvel.

One night the firm's Braintree mill caught fire. We were very annoyed that we weren't wakened up to see it. Half the mill was burnt down, but the other half was saved by a sailor who climbed on the roof. The fire brigade went on pumping splendidly until the beer ran out. After that the place was left to its fate.

At school the war passed on the whole quite peacefully. All the masters joined up and we had to have mistresses, much to our indignation. Considering there was no rationing, old Browne fed us very well; I fared much better in those days than later at Charterhouse. Blimps used often to fly over the school on their way to try to bomb U-boats, and one day when we were out for a run on the Downs we saw a ship sinking off Beachy Head. Destroyers rushed over the horizon to her rescue in clouds of smoke, but they could do nothing and finally she sank.

Browne used to conduct the service, preach the sermon, read the lesson and play the organ at school chapel. I remember him once explaining the Trinity. "You need not be worried about the Trinity," said LRB, "it is all quite simple, just the same as the wicket. Off stump Jesus Christ, middle stump God the Father, leg stump the Holy Ghost. There you are—Three in One and One in Three."

During the war, my family moved to The Howe, Halstead, which was now my home. With three children, Little Bradfords had become too small. My father looked at various houses, but he always said they were too big. He therefore chose The Howe and then had to build on to it. I remember that the first thing I did when we settled in was to make a harbour on the pond for my model destroyer. With the help of my governess, I made a chart of the pond which was framed and hung in the schoolroom. The next major operation was constructing a dug-out in the park, air raids being then the fashion. The garden boy had been a bricklayer, and with his help we put in a cooking stove. My parents came to lunch and we had some wonderful food cooked by our governess, who was French. The only drawback was that you could see neither mademoiselle nor the food for the smoke. All the same, the dug-out was voted a great success, though, needless to say, no one ever went into it during an air raid.

This was the time of the Zepps. The pheasants used to give warning of them long before we could hear them. One day a Zepp came so low over the keeper's cottage that he said he could have shot it with his gun. Another time, when we were at Frinton, one came down on the marshes. The crew all got out and, having set it on fire, surrendered to an old couple living in a cottage near by. Next day we went to look at the Zepp; the huge skeleton, lying like a dead monster in the field, was an amazing sight.

Once I had the thrill of seeing a real aeroplane. It was on the golf course at Frinton, where the pilot had flown to have a round with a friend. When he was due to take off, I watched from the sea-wall. The pilot's friend kept on turning the propeller, but the engine would not start. Finally, the pilot got out to do it himself and his friend took his place in the cockpit. Suddenly the plane started and began to rush away across the links. The pilot ran after it, shouting instructions which the other man could not hear. In the end, the machine went through a hedge and turned over on its back. Souvenirs were a great thing then: I collected a large piece of the propeller.

Towards the end of my time at St. Christopher's, there was the episode of entering for the Navy. On the advice of his first cousin, Jack Savill, my father put my name down to go for interview in 1918. (Captain Savill had been drowned when his ship, the *Hampshire*, went down with Kitchener off the west coast of Orkney.) As the Board was to take place soon after term began, I did not go back to school—unfortunately, as I heard from the Headmaster later, for they could have given me some helpful tips. After staying at Brown's Hotel, I walked with my father to the Admiralty and was straightway given a medical examination. That seemed to go all right. I was then taken into a room where I was to settle down to write an essay. Since I knew quite a bit about the Navy and the name and armament of every ship in it, as well as all the lighthouses round the coast of Britain, I was not unduly worried. But when I saw the subject I was supposed to write about, I shook with horror; it was "The Public School System".

Before I could think of a thing to say, I was summoned in to the dreaded interview. I found myself confronted by a number of elderly gentlemen, some of them probably Admirals. They asked me, I remember, about Mesopotamia, and what crops were grown in Essex. They also seemed interested in how the *Hampshire* was lost. I said "Mine", which I think was right, and having got out of that I went back to my essay, but the paper—a complete blank—had been taken away. So it was not surprising when, a few weeks later, old Browne came into my form and handed me a curt notice from the Admiralty that Their Lordships had no use for my services. I am afraid I burst into tears, but neither the mistress nor the boys in the form took any notice.

Then came Charterhouse. My father took me down, as he was an old Carthusian himself. I was entered for Gownboys, which was my father's old house. My house master was a nice fellow but had a predilection for Games Captains, and, as I was never any good at games, he was naturally not too pleased at having me wished on him. Luckily for me, the housemaster's nephew, Cecil Mould, was a fellow culprit; we became great buddies. Charterhouse had, of course, been a monastery before the Reformation. To all intents and purposes, it still was. The headmaster was Frank Fletcher. I only remember speaking to him twice. Once was when he beat me so that I could go and shoot against Marlborough instead of being kept in. The second time was when I said goodbye on leaving. He said, "Well, good-bye, you scoundrel."

The masters were, of course, our natural enemies, but some I remember with affection. One was the Reverend Selby-Lowndes, whose bent back was popularly attributed to service in the Foreign Legion—in all probability, this was legend.

The whole aim and object in our House was winning cups. In the end, we got the lot. I helped to bag the Shooting Cup, but that was my sole contribution.

Even after the end of the war, the food was awful; we had to supplement it from the tuck-shop and the Army and Navy Stores at Aldershot. On one occasion, the edict went forth that too much bread was being eaten and that toasting was to stop: We decided to see what we could do about this and the word was passed round to eat as much bread as possible without toasting. The house average was eighteen rounds, the maximum twenty-four. That night after prayers, the housemaster exploded: "Pigs, PIGS, *PIGS!*" he roared. He threatened to beat every boy in the house, found this impracticable and proceeded to beat the eleven ringleaders instead. He found it very hard work.

The house was run by monitors, who could have you beaten by the head of the house for any reason, or none. The easiest crime was being "a general nuisance". Appeal to the housemaster was quite useless; he always said he had to support authority. These "executions" were quite a thing. You were told to fetch a straight-backed chair, all the monitors of the house were present, and the head boy took a run, the full length of the room. You got six or eight strokes of the cane. We were unlucky enough to suffer under one of those clever fellows who had got into the sixth young. He was an expert racquets player, and by the time he had had a term or two's practice he could land six strokes on the same spot with unerring accuracy. After one such beating you didn't want another that term.

One Sunday while I was at Charterhouse we had a magnificent fire. We were in our form doing scripture when the alarm went and all rushed out to find that Lockites, one of the school houses, was blazing. As the house stood below the level of "Big Ground", we had a wonderful view. Soon we were all roped in to man the school fire engine. About twenty boys stood on each side and pulled the bars up and down. The roof was burning splendidly, and we watched the school fire brigade, under the captain of football, doing valiant work squirting water on to what remained of it. After a time, the official Guildford brigade turned up, got on the roof and proceeded to order our brigade off it. The school brigade then turned their hoses on the Guildford firemen. Eventually the top storey was burnt down.

My memory of Charterhouse is that my time was mostly taken up with extra work, extra drill and beatings, but there were other incidents of one kind and another. When I was about sixteen I had a dose of rheumatic fever. After a bit I was removed to sick quarters, where I lay for some weeks and was (so I heard afterwards) prayed for in chapel. Later, on the advice of our family doctor, my father had me taken home by ambulance. There, looked after by a professional nurse and rationed to one baked apple a day, I very soon recovered.

One amusing episode comes back to me. I was late for early school after a great rush and was called up by my form master. "I don't think you have washed this morning," said he. I looked at him and replied, "No, sir! And I don't think you have shaved."

Games, of course, were compulsory. Football was mostly a matter of being knocked about. Cricket was worse because it lasted longer. I was never put on to bowl and used to spend most of my time fielding, chewing a piece of grass at the edge of the field. Generally I was near the bottom of the batting order and the game was over before I could go in.

The "Corps" was also compulsory. Polishing one's leather equipment and brass buckles with a stuff called "ox blood" was one of the main activities. On parade, which took place three times a week, we spent most of our time forming fours and other such drill. Sometimes we went out on manœuvres. The service rifle was too heavy for the smaller boys, who spent their time being sick in the hedge, and generally the bigger ones marched carrying six rifles.

Once we attacked a hill and captured the Harrow lunch. On that occasion we were armed with blank cartridges. On another we shot the umpire's horse with date stones, which we found fitted the barrel of a service rifle and went to perfection with a blank cartridge behind them. This was great fun. The annual camp on Salisbury Plain took place in the summer holidays—this was compulsory, too, of course. We lived in army bell-tents, slept on "donkey's breakfasts" (straw palliasses), and spent most of our time washing up. Once, before my day, Charterhouse was camped next to Harrow. One night they cut our tent ropes. Charterhouse turned out with bayonets and mallets and tradition has it that several people were killed.

In order to get out of cricket, I took up shooting and eventually got in the eight. This meant I was a "blood", privileged to wear grey flannel trousers and go to the "bloods' window" at the tuckshop. We used to do our shooting practice under the instruction of our sergeant-major at Puttenham. Once we won the Rapid and Snap at Bisley and returned with a big trophy.

One splendid thing happened during my school days: a performance of the "Masque", the history of Charterhouse in the form of a play, which is acted by the masters and boys every five years. It showed the monks being turned out of their monastery, Lovelace and Thackeray reading their words, Havelock relieving Lucknow.

I remember well how old Selby-Lowndes told us once that we were to do Horace, Book I, the following term. My father taught it me all the holidays until I knew it by heart. The first day of term we were told that we were going to do Cicero for School Certificate: Horace was out. Cuthbert Williams, who was also trying get into Cambridge, used to go down with me to Selby-Lowndes. There in the evenings we waded through Cicero. Eventually we got through the "Little Go", for which he had tutored us, as well as the Trinity Entrance Examination.

In those years I made two pals who have been my friends all my life' Geoffrey Marks and Guy Wreford-Brown, son of the famous footballer. After leaving school, Guy, Geoffrey and I decided to do a bicycle tour of the Highlands. We started from Struan, where my father had a moor, and went via Loch Laggan to Fort William. We were throwing stones in the loch one day when an old boy with a white beard came and threatened us with arrest for throwing stones on the Sabbath.

We went on by the Pass of Glencoe and eventually to Loch Lomond. This was before the days of arterial roads, so we found the hills very steep; we had to push both up and down them as our brakes weren't good enough. At Loch Lomond we arrived at a large hotel inhabited by dinner jackets: we ate a bun in the summerhouse. We were always running out of money since the hotels were much more expensive than we had been told, but we got ourselves over the Pass of Killiecrankie and so home.

August Courtauld (back left) in the Charterhouse Shooting Team.

3

Cambridge

I N OCTOBER 1923 I went up to Trinity College, Cambridge, armed with many instructions from home about not getting into the hands of the Jews, etc. I had lodgings in Jesus Lane, rooms that smelt appallingly of cabbage boiled in the basement. Next door was a church which used to make a dreadful racket on three bells. However, there were two very nice inmates, Bill Corbett and "Goose" Gosling. They have remained my friends ever since.

I found the freedom of Cambridge a great change after Charterhouse. Deciding I would like to read something different from the subjects I had done at school, I took Engineering. The trouble was that I hadn't done enough maths at school to pass the qualifying examination for the Tripos or Honours Degree, I therefore read for the ordinary degree, which was in fact much more practical and interesting. In those days there was not the emphasis on work there is now. Some people did military subjects with only one lecture a term and no examination! Engineering, unfortunately, had a lot of lectures and I had to turn up at 9 a.m. every morning. But there was no work in the afternoons; then we would take our dogs out or go beagling. Sometimes we used to go wildfowling on the Fens or the Essex marshes. Once we went to walk over the Saltings near Bradwell with Linnett, the professional wildfowler, who lived near the old chapel of St. Peter's-on-the-Wall. It was a lovely day, much too fine for wildfowling, but it was splendid looking over the wide marshes to the sea far away. Another time we thought we would go spratting at Brightlingsea and went out in one of the old sailing smacks to catch our sprats some way out at sea. It was fascinating to see how the men managed their nets and a wonderful sight when a net was hauled up full of sprats which flowed like a stream of quicksilver into the fish-hold.

Some fellows used to keep hunters with the Fitzwilliam or other fashionable packs. I occasionally used to have a day with the East Essex, or a day's shooting with my father at home. When I went hunting I used to ride hirelings. Once, on one of these, I was trying to open a gate; the horse took a jump at the gate. I landed on my nose in the road, and all the field filed past. When they had all gone, I got on again and started home. I found my nose was broken. It seemed a very long ride.

I joined a cavalry squadron and we used to do drill on hired horses before breakfast. There was tent-pegging, with swords and lances, though I generally had to leave before that, to go to my lectures. One day there was to be an inspection of the whole of the Cambridge OTC; the GOC London District was to come down to do it. Bobby Perkins (a well-known figure) sent the Colonel at Cambridge a telegram from a remote post office on the route from London saying that the General had broken down and would be unable to undertake the inspection. The parade was accordingly dismissed, and the General arrived to find only a few parents and the Vice-Chancellor on view.

Most people seemed to belong to one of the two Clubs, the Pitt or the Athenaeum. I never did myself. The Athenaeum was considered the élite. I once asked what they did there. I was told, "Oh, they scratch their dogs."

One Guy Fawkes night, I attached a firework to the top of a lamp post and descended into the arms of a policeman. Appearing in the dock, I was just going to be fined the usual five shillings when there was a hold-up in the proceedings. The Chairman of the Bench was having a whispered argument with the woman sitting next to him. I recognized her as a vague cousin, a would-be Socialist MP Eventually the fine was announced. It was two pounds.

Goose (Billy Gosling) and I once thought we would see what happened if we starved. We therefore ate nothing at all for three days, and then ordered ourselves a wonderful dinner to be brought up from the College kitchen. It ended with a magnificent treacle pudding. Afterwards I found myself rolling in agony on the floor.

As part of my degree course, I was detailed, one long vacation, to go and work at an engineering factory. I went to the British Thomson-Houston works at Rugby. There I lived in digs, which cost three guineas a week. My pay was eighteen shillings, with various deductions for breakages, overalls, etc. I worked in the apprentice department, and the first job I had was to turn forty-six feet of gas pipe into small pieces on a lathe according to a blueprint. I finished this in a fortnight and asked the foreman what I should do next. He said, "Go and get some more gas pipe."

During my time at Cambridge my father gave me a small racing boat, the first *Duet*. She was one of the well-known ex-24-footer class, and I used to go down to Burnham on Saturday afternoons to race her. All the boats in the class were different and they used to race on handicap. If you did badly one day, you got a good handicap the next. I had a hand called Ted Bourne who looked like an elderly chimpanzee. He was very strong, with long arms, and nimble as a cat; he was up and down the mast of this little boat before you could say Jack Robinson. But he would stand no nonsense. Once a man who was having a friendly "touch up", as we call it, on a Sunday, asked Ted to set the spinnaker. "There ain't no prize money," he said, and jumped overboard to swim ashore.

This was the time of the great rags. A society called the Caius Co-optimists organized these. One was "Tutankhamen's Tomb", in which Tutankhamen emerged from the gents' lavatory in Market Square with great applause. Another was the taking of a famous statue from King's College, London. Detectives actually got to the room where it was but never found it. An even more difficult operation was the removal of a large German gun from Jesus to Caius. For days beforehand, a party had been cutting through the college railings. On the night of the operation, a diversion was caused by an organized disturbance at the other end of the town. This drew away the Proctors and the Police. The railings were then removed and the gun hauled to Caius, where it was found safely installed next morning. There were other rags. One was an "invitation" to all the black men of Cambridge to go to breakfast with the Master of Trinity in their surplices. It is not revealed what the Master (J. J. Thomson) had to say when they arrived. There was also the occasion when someone let the grazing of Trinity Great Court to the Fair on Midsummer Common for their elephants. Luckily for Trinity, the elephants couldn't get through the Great Gate.

In my last year at Trinity, I moved into College and had very nice rooms in Great Court, facing Hall. Dogs were not allowed in College, so we decided to have a dogs' tea party in my rooms. Our dogs were hauled up through the window in suitcases and cricket bags from outside. When the college porter came with some letters, his face was a picture. My dog Rover habitually lived in my rooms, entering by the same route.

I was roped into attending the Trinity Ball, which happened during May Week on the Backs. It was a delightful summer evening and I strolled with my partner along the river. Suddenly she turned to me and said, "This is too awful. Can't you think of anything to say?" In fact I had no use for girls at this time and thought them a nuisance. I never really saw one at close quarters until I became engaged some years later.

The day after the Ball, Bill Corbett and I decided to drive down to his home in Shropshire. We arrived in our white ties and tails for lunch. His father seemed a bit astonished.

Exams were a chancy thing. It was said there was a don in Kings who used to take all the exam papers up to the top of his staircase and throw them down when he was examining for the classical Tripos. Those that only got to the next floor got a Third, the ones that reached the first floor a Second, while the few that managed to get to the bottom scored a First.

After getting our exams over, Bill, Goose, Charles de Bunsen and I thought we would go for a cruise. Before going down I had built a boat at Lymington. She was called *Hallowe'en* and was one of the new West Solent Restricted Class. The 24-footers were finished and it was decided to start this class at Burnham. In March, with one or two friends, I sailed *Hallowe'en* round to Burnham: she was about seven tons and had a little cabin and foc'sle, so she made quite a good little cruiser.

We left Ramsgate before dawn, having picked up Goose on the pierhead. Ostend sounded a good place to us, as it had a Casino. We hadn't any charts, but what matter? The wind was fair, but about half-way over it came on to blow. We got the mainsail down with difficulty and ran the rest of the way under the foresail. Later we heard that the Ruytingen lightship had reported the passing of a yacht out of control. A passenger steamer came along to ask if we needed help. We held beer bottles up to our ears and carried on. When we got to the other side, there seemed to be no sign of Ostend, only miles of sand dunes. So we tossed up which way to turn, and after sailing a few miles North, we got there. After berthing, the Customs came aboard to ask for our papers. As we hadn't got any, we gave them a glass of sherry instead. This seemed to go down quite well. Apart from one of the crew falling off the quay into the harbour one night when we were coming back from the casino, our jaunt went according to plan. I remember going ashore to get some grub. Summoning up my best French, I said to a woman scrubbing her doorstep in front of her shop, *"Avez-vous des oeufs?"* She replied in English, "What do you want?" We then sent Goose ashore to try his luck. He advanced on a shop, mustered his best French and asked, *"Avez-vous de cochin?"* The reply was "No sir, but you can have either bacon or ham." We sailed back safely, and Goose made a wonderful sardine omelette out of the *oeufs*. My father and mother gave a coming-out dance for Betty at their house in London; something quite new for them, as they didn't go in for social occasions. The dance was a great success except that during the evening Betty found the drawing-room entirely populated by girls. Bill and I had fixed up a bar in the cellar and laid on beer. No-one found us.

August Courtauld in his room in Cambridge.

4

Lapland

THE LONG vacations were fun. There were people who stayed up at Cambridge and worked, but most of us went off where the spirit moved us. One December I departed with some friends to North Uist for wildfowl and mice. Chaworth-Musters was keen to catch the local mouse; the rest of us concentrated on geese, widgeon, woodcock and snipe. We lived at the hotel on what we shot; I remember we got sixty-five snipe on Christmas Day.

Another time, after the Cavalry camp, my first cousin George (who was up at Pembroke) and I decided to go to Lapland. We took passage in a funny little old-fashioned steamer from Hull and landed at Helsinki in Finland. There we saw six policemen trying to suppress a very large, very drunk Finn on the quay: he threw them away as if they were little cats. For this trip my father gave me a flask of pineapple rum which had come from my grandfather's cellar. This was very popular, especially with the old salts.

We visited Lake Ladoga on the Russian frontier—the biggest lake in Europe and the island of Valamo in the middle of it, entirely populated by Russian monks. It was curious to see these monks, in their tall hats and long beards, manning the little steamer which took us out to the island. We stayed at the monastery in a cell and found the services most impressive, with a wonderful hidden choir. The food was so covered with flies that you couldn't see it. However, the lake bathing was something we did enjoy. At one house in Finland where we stayed there was a tame pig, most affectionate and very clean. He always came in at meal-times to be scratched.

After going up through the lakes by steamer and seeing various castles, we travelled by bus from Rovaniemi on the Arctic Circle to Lake Inari in Lapland. There we went fishing, caught quite a lot of trout and grayling, and saw something of the Lapps. The worst thing was the mosquitoes, but we covered our faces and hands with a mixture of equal parts of Stockholm tar and olive oil and found that pretty effective. One night we made ourselves at home in an empty Lapp hut and went to sleep. Towards morning the Lapp came in to cook himself a meal. He did not seem surprised to see us and was a nice cheerful little man.

There came a day when we thought it was time we had a bath. When we had given notice of this, great stones were heated up and an old woman took us into the bath hut. She proceeded to put water on the hot stones; the whole place filled with steam, and as the hut was hermetically sealed we were very soon gasping for breath. When the steam died down, we broke out into a great sweat, and the old woman then beat us lightly with a birch broom. We emerged from all this much refreshed. It was quite the best bath I have ever had.

We left the country from Kirkenes, taking passage in a Norwegian steamer. After passing Vadsö and Vardö, we rounded the North Cape, where I celebrated my twenty-first birthday. We could smell Vadsö and Vardö long before we could see them. The smell came from vast quantities of cod hung out to dry, for sale later all over Europe as salt fish. On the way down the west coast of Norway, we called at Hammerfest, Tromsö and many other places, eventually arriving at Bergen, where we took a ship for Newcastle. This was the first real travelling I had done abroad. I enjoyed it.

5

With Wordie to Greenland

Aꜰᴛᴇʀ ᴛᴀᴋɪɴɢ my degree (two years Engineering and one year Geography) in 1926, I decided I must go to the Arctic. Enquiries revealed that you could go on hunting parties to Spitzbergen. But eventually I discovered a tower in St. John's College surmounted by James Wordie. He had been with Shackleton in the Antarctic, where their ship, the *Endurance*, was crushed in the ice. They had hauled their boats across the ice to Elephant Island, where they lived under an up-turned boat until Shackleton sailed to South Georgia to get relief. Wordie very kindly invited me to go with him to East Greenland. The main object was to take gravity readings at the place where this had been done a century before.

We sailed from Aberdeen in a small Norwegian sealer, the *Heimland*. Lars Jakobsen was the captain, and the crew were, of course, all Norwegians. There were eight members of the expedition, among them my friend Charles de Bunsen. He had been at Marlborough before Cambridge and we both agreed we would rather go to quod than back to our respective schools.

Calling at Reykjavik for coal, we sailed westward. One day the sea died down and we found ourselves in the pack-ice. Great white floes floated on every side, with the sea gently lapping the blue edges. Far to the west was the lovely Alpine skyline of East Greenland. The Captain was in the crow's nest with his big telescope, shouting down his orders to the wheelhouse as we twisted and turned this way and that to get through the pack. Sometimes the ship would strike a floe with a heavy bump; at other times the propeller would hit the ice with a jar and the engine had to be stopped immediately.

Now and then we could get no further and had to make fast to a floe with ice anchors. This was a chance for hunting. We got a number of seals and once, from the boat, a huge bull walrus. We also shot one or two bears, those most beautiful creatures.

While we were held up like this, the mate used to go on the ice with his sextant and a bowl of engine oil to fix our position. By reflecting the sun in the oil he could get the altitude with his sextant. Gordon Manley, who was in charge of the gravity observations, was doing the same thing one day with a theodolite when we saw a big bear coming quietly up behind him. We let it get fairly close and then yelled. His surprise was glorious to see.

After some weeks, we got through the pack to the coast and a closer view of the magnificent mountains. We wended our way up East Greenland to the Pendulum Islands where we were to take the gravity observations. Gordon Manley had brought some gold pendulums from Cambridge for the purpose. They were so precious that he had to sleep with them under his pillow. We soon had his gear ashore and pitched two tents. There he had to spend about a week watching these pendulums swinging day and night and also taking sights for latitude, longitude and time. When he had finished, we resumed our exploration of the fjords. We went up the great Franz Josef Fjord to its head, passing the splendid Devil's Castle and the wonderful stratified cliffs which line this inlet. They look like a great wedge of chocolate and cream cake.

When we got to the head of the fjord, we went for a climbing excursion. The idea was to try and get to the famous Petermann Peak, which was supposed to be 14,000 feet. We found ourselves scrambling up scree where for every two feet we climbed we slipped back one. It all seemed very hard work and our loads were heavy. Eventually we discovered that the peak was many miles inland and that we should have neither the time nor the food to reach it. After a few days we returned to the ship, delighted to get some good meals again: everything we had eaten on the trip tasted of paraffin which had leaked out into our rucksacks.

Once he had got into his kilt and tam-o'-shanter, Wordie was indefatigable. He was keen to go ashore on all possible occasions with his geological hammer to have a "look see", and it was always a privilege to go with him, for he was the best of company. I remember once trying to help him make a map with lavatory paper.

Norwegians are great hunters but have an insatiable blood lust. They are very good shots with a rifle and have to kill everything they see. On one occasion we sighted a herd of musk-oxen; the whole crew landed and while the herd formed a ring to defend their calves, the whole lot was killed. One of the calves was brought back on board and we became very fond of it. The musk-ox has a very large and heavy head and when this little calf took people behind the legs it generally knocked them down on to the deck. Maggie as we called her—had another playful habit, which was to station herself outside the ship's heads and stop anyone who happened to be in there from coming out. Once she imprisoned the Captain, who was an enormous man, and he was stuck there for a very long time. We put Maggie in Gordon Manley's cabin one day; she kept him in order for quite a while.

Later we captured a polar bear cub, Susie, whose mother had been shot. Susie was nailed down in a strong wooden box on deck. On the way home we struck a heavy gale and there was a big sea running. Sounds of hammering were heard in the night. We discovered that the cub had got a paw through her box and was breaking out. Near Iceland the mate came down one night and reported "Bear and musk-ox not good." Evidently they were sea-sick, so we put into the nearest fjord in Iceland for them to recover. When we got back to Aberdeen, both found their way to the zoo. The keepers were afraid of Maggie, who used to charge them, and she didn't last very long. Susie remained there until quite recently. She would never take a mate.

One day when we were at anchor in the fjords, the famous Dr. Lauge Koch came to see us. He was standing up in his boat smoking a cigar. He told us of an English boy who had died not long before, I think from scurvy (he would eat nothing but tinned food), and said that the Arctic always claimed a victim every year.

After his first expedition to Greenland, Courtauld (centre) travelled to the Sahara with the brothers Peter and Francis Rodd (left and right respectively).

6

The Sahara

I N THE spring of 1927, I set off with the brothers Francis and
Peter Rodd for the Mountains of Aïr in the Sahara. We went
by ship to Lagos and thence three days by train to Kano. This
was a fine old city, built entirely of mud and with a mud wall twelve
miles long surrounding it. After that we went north to Katsina,
where we bought our camels from the Emir.

The expedition consisted of the three of us and about twelve men.
One of these was Tchekmedin, a Tuareg of the People of the Veil.
We had a Fulani cook and his boy and a Hausa servant for each of us.
Thirty camels carried our gear, our water and ourselves. We were a
well-armed party and had no need to fear trouble from raiders, since
we had rifles for all our men and plenty of ammunition. Slowly we
rode north towards the mountain oasis of Aïr. It was very hot and
at the beginning we suffered a good deal from thirst. After a time
we trained ourselves not to drink at all during the day and make up
for this by hot cups of tea without milk when we got into camp. It
is mostly flat bush country bordering on the desert, with dead trees
waving blackened arms to a brazen sky.

After some weeks we reached the Aïr group of mountains rising
to 6,000 feet; it is a lovely country, with fine valleys full of good
pasture. It was our practice to travel on from well to well. At each
we would water our camels, fill our water skins, and at night fix our
position by the stars. After more travelling we reached the French
fort of Agades—a "Beau Geste" affair with French officers and black
Senegalese troops. We thought it strange how empty this splendid
country was, but soon found the explanation: a camel corps setting

out on patrol, splendidly mounted with an armament of machine guns and escorted by Goums, or local scouts.

We had diplomatic permits from Paris and asked the Commandant of the Fort for permission to go north to Tripoli and the Mediterranean. He said that of course we could go anywhere we liked, but that as there was trouble on up there, he advised us to change our plans. And the French warned us the Tuareg were treacherous and would stab you in the back if they got the chance.

The next thing that happened was that our guide, Tchekmedin, was arrested. We went to the Fort to investigate and were told he had been found talking against the French in the village. We had to pay quite a lot of francs to get him out. This did not seem a very healthy place for us, so we decided to move to the north of Aïr to fit ourselves out for the journey to Tripoli—for, needless to say, we were still going.

We spent the rainy season near the village of Auderas, living in great comfort on dates and camel's milk cheeses. One day I went out with my Hausa on foot to try to get something for the pot. On the way back I felt thirsty and drank from a stagnant pool, in spite of my Hausa's warnings. As a result of this I had a severe attack of dysentery and lay day after day in a tent, unable to move and getting steadily weaker. In the end Francis thought he'd better do something about it and gave me an injection of emetine. This had a wonderful effect; by the next day I was up and about again.

In the rains, the barren valleys blossomed into a splendid green. The wadis ran with water for the only time in the whole year. Every afternoon there was a tremendous thunderstorm. Sometimes we got two inches of rain in an hour; this sounded like a bombardment and it was impossible to hear anything else while it was going on. We had to be careful that our camels did not eat too much of the lush grass. If they did, they got blood to the head; the cure for this was putting snuff up their noses. Once in a while, too, a bull camel would go "must". Then he was dangerous.

Peter and I climbed the local mountain with the idea of doing some mapping: But when we got to the top, which was about 6,000 feet, it was so hazy we could see nothing. The usual thunderstorm then came on and we sheltered beneath a distinctly inadequate bush. Coming down had its difficulties since my sandals broke and the rock was too hot to walk on with bare feet.

Francis used to doctor the camels as well as the men, draw the maps, take the stars and find the water. Peter looked after the food and spoke the languages. He had a fine ear for tongues and very soon learnt to cope with Tuareg as well as Arabic. He already knew most of the European languages and conversed happily in French or Italian as the case demanded. I did little but help with the mapping, the star sights and keeping the peace. My most important duty was to wind the chronometer each day and rate it by time signals from Rugby on our special Marconi sand-proof long-wave set. Conversations round the camp table in the evening were too erudite for me. Mostly they seemed to be about personalities in London of whom I had never heard, or Greek history, or the origin of words. One subject which, as in the Arctic, was never discussed was the climate.

After the rains we set off for the extreme north of the mountains, camping by a remote well which was a likely place for raiders. We took our turns keeping watch by the well each night, one at a time. It was an eerie job sitting on the rocks, rifle on knees, listening to the sounds of the desert. The hyenas screamed, the jackals howled, and it was seldom still.

By and by our Tuaregs announced that they did not want to go with us to the north; they said they would be shot when they came back. We therefore decided to strike west across the desert to the Niger. It was unknown country and the position of the wells was uncertain, but we took on a guide called Khayar, nicknamed "Higher the fewer". He had been that way ten years before and thought he knew it.

Before we set out in earnest on the westward journey, we did a bit of exploring round about. Our riding camels were mountain beasts and could go up rocky hills at a trot. We used to carry with us only our rifles, a little food and a blanket. Lightly laden like this, we used to cover quite a lot of ground. After trotting all day, we would have a meal of the famous kus-kus, a dish of wheat much favoured by the Arabs. Having eaten this on the sand, we rolled ourselves each in his blanket for the night. It used to get mighty cold after the sun set; the temperature fell some 30° in an hour. Once, in the desert, we came across a pool with rock sides and bathed there, which was delicious after the heat of the day. On the rock we found inscribed the most amazing drawings: women in breeches, and animals such as elephants which had not been known in that part of the world in historic times.

The heat returned after the rains and we used to get 115° in the shade. In camp we used put camel's milk into old wine bottles given us by the French; in the morning it had solidified and gone sour— very good to eat with our porridge.

At length we set out for the Niger and home, "Higher the fewer" riding in front, the caravan in a long line behind him, and we three riding or walking as we felt inclined. The speed was two and a half miles an hour. Peter used to knit on the march. I would work out the star observations—I carried the Nautical Almanac in one saddle bag and the log tables in the other—and I also kept the route book, riding behind the caravan, checking the course with a compass and making an estimate of the speed. I never found that "Higher the fewer" deviated a single degree from his course so long as the sun or stars were shining. The wells were mostly about a hundred miles apart: it generally took us five days to get from one to another. When we got there, we usually found a deep hole bored through the rock, with grooves made on the side by the ropes of countless centuries. Our men had to draw the water for our camels with skin buckets lowered down the well. The camels needed about twenty gallons apiece, and after that there were our water skins to fill. These were made of goat-skin and the new ones stank. The scene at the well was truly Biblical: men, women and children were around, there were herds and flocks of camels, sheep and goats coming to water, and the odd man on a donkey. The country, of hard sand or gravel, was completely flat and entirely featureless, and it is a mystery how we found the wells without any landmarks.

Our camels were loaded with food, water, surveying instruments and medical stores. There was also the odd hen dangling alive by its legs from the cook's saddle; dead animals don't last long in that country. Before dawn a boy was sent out to bring in the camels which had been grazing all night. After breakfast, during which the camels were loaded, we would get under way. It was pleasant enough then, at about six o'clock, and remained so until nine or thereabouts, when the sun began to beat down. Sometimes a Tuareg would sit his camel down so that he could dismount and say his prayers. It used to take him a long time to catch up; the caravan never stopped. We had no meal until supper, after dark. Our camp was chosen according to the pasture—a few thorn bushes or some "hadh" were what the camels liked best. An incredible number of insects gathered at our candle-lantern while we ate. Scorpions, tarantulas, praying mantis and grasshoppers seemed the most common. Sometimes in daytime we would spot a sand-viper. Our men rushed at it with their swords, but always it disappeared down a hole. Once a viper glided under my bare feet as I sat at the camp table. Luckily Peter saw it and said, "Put your feet up—quick!" There were also immense ants which bit like fury. Sometimes we would shoot a gazelle, an addax antelope or oryx for the pot.

Eventually we reached the banks of the Niger. Here, at Burem, it is a noble stream running through the bare desert. After paying off our men and selling or giving away the camels, we took a motor boat up the river bound for Timbuctoo and Dakar. There were many channels through great beds of reeds, and as our pilot did not seem to know the river any better than we did, we were forever taking the wrong turning and getting stuck. Hippo and crocodile were plentiful in the river or on its banks. We did not like to go too near the hippo since they had a reputation for getting under a boat to capsize it, pushing the occupants to the bottom and sitting on them.

After many days we got to Dakar and took ship in a cargo boat for England. In the mouth of the Channel we got into a gale and were hove-to for four days. We saw the old *Mauretania* rolling home. One moment you would see the whole of her bare decks and the next, her bottom. We finally got to Liverpool several days late.

It was Spring 1928 when I got back from Africa, and I was carted off by my parents, with Betty, to the Riviera. The idea was that I should become civilized. We stayed at an hotel which was completely English. Its merit was that it contained Rudyard Kipling. He and my father used to discuss Horace. It was a great privilege being able to talk to the Master; I shall never forget his bright eyes. After a week I could find nothing more to see on the Riviera, so I travelled home third class to sail my boat.

7

The City

B Y THE time I got back from Africa, my father seemed to think that I ought to learn something about "business" and "settle down". So he got me into Francis Rodd's stockbroking firm of Buckmaster and Moore, where I was taken on at a salary of one hundred and fifty pounds a year and made a "red button". This meant that I had to wander round the City delivering papers but was not allowed to enter the sacred Stock Exchange itself. For some time things went on fairly peacefully; then the great boom of 1929 came, and up till ten o'clock every night we were working to get through a mass of transfers.

Our firm was run by a financial genius who employed a battery of scientists and worked out with graphs what was going to happen in finance. Unfortunately he could not foretell when it was going to happen. Much to their disgust, our clients found themselves being taken out of all their shares in the middle of the boom. The slump which he had foretold happened, of course, but a year later.

At this time I thought I would learn how to fly. After office hours I used to go by tube to Stag Lane, and then, when the weather was suitable, took the air in a Gypsy Moth, accompanied by an instructor. We were powered by a hundred horse-power engine and our maximum speed was eighty miles an hour. The cockpit was open and it was very noisy. One had to look at a spring indicator on the wing to find one's speed. There was a red mark at 40 mph; if the speed fell below this, one stalled. As a contrast to the City, it was all great fun.

After a time I was transferred to the "Box". This was a small office by one of the doors into "the House", or Stock Exchange. It was most amusing watching the street market after "the House" was shut. My job was to take orders on the telephone from the office and pass them to the dealers for execution. One day I took down from the girl at the other end, "Invest forty-five thousand pounds in Imperial Chemicals". Next time he came in, I passed this to the dealer. He queried it and said it seemed rather a lot; however, I told him it was all right and he'd better get on with it. After an interval, the deal came through and I reported it to the office by telephone. *"What!"* came back. "Isn't it all right?" said I. "No, you fool. I said invest forty-five pounds, not thousands." It appeared this deal was for a small butcher in Southend. Panic ensued. The partners came down in their top hats and said they must undo it if they could. I suggested they might hold on to it, as the shares were going up, but they said that wouldn't do at all and disappeared into "the House" to try some unscrambling.

I did not last much longer in the "Box", or in the firm either, for that matter. I told them that I wanted to go to Greenland again, and they made no attempt to dissuade me.

8

Petermann Peak

AFTER LEAVING the City I went to stay at the Ilchester Arms at Abbotsbury, in Dorset. The party consisted of Ralph Bingham, Peter Rodd, Mollie my future wife, and Betty. Mollie and Betty shared one bed, Peter and I another. We did a lot of pub-crawling over the Downs and paid many visits to the famous Tithe Barn and Swannery. Ralph, who was keen on etching at the time, made a sketch of the Tithe Barn. I remember he also astonished us by saying that the three years he spent in the trenches with the Coldstream Guards were the best three years of his life.

In the summer of 1929 I set out again with James Wordie for East Greenland. Our main object was to try and climb Petermann, which we had seen in the distance on the previous expedition. We had the same ship, the *Heimland*, and the same captain, Lars Jakobsen. Unfortunately, it was a bad ice year. We spent three weeks getting through the pack and finally became utterly immobile. We tried dynamite, but it did not seem to make any difference. Day after day went by: the sun shone, but we could not move. All the time we could see the splendid mountains of Greenland in the west. We and the pack were drifting south at the rate of about ten miles a day. When we finally got through, we had only a short summer left to us.

Again we went up to the head of the Franz Josef Fjord. We landed and started our climbing journey, carrying our food, tents and sleeping bags on our backs. After crossing many ranges, we eventually got to the top of Petermann. "Bunny" Fuchs—now leading the Transantarctic Expedition—and I spent quite a time sheltering behind a rock to boil the thermometer. This, after calculation, gave us the height of the peak. It turned out to be 9,300 feet and not 14,000, as the maps had it.

We named a number of hitherto unknown mountains on our way. These included Gog and Magog, after the little hills near Cambridge. After an eighteen hour march, we reached the ship again, thankful to get some good food.

On the return voyage we visited Captain Mikkelson at his whaling station on the Faeroes, which stank to high heaven.

We came back to England in high spirits. We had got our Peak.

Sir James Mann Wordie.

9

Gino's Expedition

The Coast

Aᶠᵗᵉʳ ᴍʏ return from Greenland I came across Gino Watkins, I can't remember how. He seemed a virile and forceful fellow. He had led his first expedition before he was twenty-one and had lately come back from a year in Labrador. Now he was planning an expedition "to explore the possibilities of an air route to Canada by the great circle". Aeroplanes in those days could not fly the Atlantic direct. Gino thought that there should be a route by the Faeroes, Iceland, Greenland and Baffinland; this would save distance and provide landing grounds. The unexplored part of this route was Greenland.

The main problem was money. Gino estimated that the expedition would cost about £8,000 and we hadn't got it. However, we both set to work. He went round the firms which could supply our needs, while I tackled the cousins and aunts. We had a great supporter in Admiral Sir William Goodenough, President of the Royal Geographical Society. The Secretary, Arthur Hinks, also helped us a lot. We had a room in the RGS on the second floor, next door to dear old Reeves, the Instructor in survey. There we concocted our plans and Gino interviewed people who wanted to come with us. We had a filing cabinet which generally contained some excellent cake, and Gino had his gramophone.

The Admiral often used to drop in to see how we were getting on. On one occasion, when we were scratching our heads over the charter of our ship, he came in and said, "Well, my boys, what are you worrying about now?" We answered, "Well, sir, we are trying to think out what deadweight tonnage is." "I can't tell you," said the Admiral, "but I'll find out." He picked up the telephone and ordered, "Give me the Admiralty." He soon got through; then, "I want the First Sea Lord. That you, First Sea Lord? This is Admiral Sir William Goodenough, President of the Royal Geographical Society. What is deadweight tonnage? ... You don't know! Thought you wouldn't." Down went the receiver. He turned to us, "You see, he doesn't know."

Firms were very generous: soon we had most of the stores we wanted given us free. The cousins and aunts also stumped up nobly. Personnel started coming along; the Navy lent us a doctor, the Army a signal officer, and the Air Force two pilots to fly our Moths. We chartered the *Quest* to take us to Greenland. Captain L. Schjelderup, a very experienced ice navigator, was her master. The *Quest* had been Sir Ernest Shackleton's ship on his last expedition to the Antarctic: he had died on board. She was to come to St. Katherine's Dock, just below the Tower Bridge, to embark us and our stores. Jamie Scott, who had been with Gino in Labrador, was sent off to West Greenland to buy fifty huskies. He was to bring them back to the Faeroes, where Captain Mikkelson would feed them on whale meat and lend us an island to keep them on.

One day old Reeves at the RGS said, "I've got the very man for you; he is working with me. He could carry the whole expedition on his shoulders." He then produced an immense fellow who turned out to be John Rymill, an Australian; he was signed on forthwith.

By the beginning of July 1930 all was ready. We had a farewell party on the dockside the evening before we sailed. George Robey entertained us, and our families and supporters came along, as well as the crew of the ship. Mollie (to whom I was now engaged) was there. Among our supporters were the Air Minister (Lord Thomson) and the Chief of the Air Staff (Sir Sefton Brancker). Both were killed soon afterwards in the crash of the R101. Gino had no one to back him at the Air Ministry when he returned.

We duly sailed from St. Katherine's Dock and then anchored off Erith to have a farewell party aboard Stephen Courtauld's new yacht, the *Virginia*. Stephen was Chairman of the Expedition Committee and a great supporter. The first thing that happened on the *Virginia* was that Percy Lemon, our signal officer, got bitten by the ship's monkey—a deep bite in the wrist which bled all over the upper deck and made an awful mess on the beautiful new planking. The captain was furious. As for Percy, it seemed he was allergic to iodine; he did not fully recover for three months. The next misadventure occurred when we were actually at sea. Our doctor developed a very bad tooth, and when we put in to Blyth to coal, he went to the dentist, who could only get it out with a hammer and chisel.

Then we went on to the Faeroes to collect the dogs. Jamie was there, in very good form. He had got a fine lot of huskies, one of whom had managed to swim away from the island and attack some sheep. The dogs were embarked and put in a pen on the foredeck. They were pretty miserable at sea, as were several members of the expedition. One man was unable to leave his bunk the whole way to Greenland.

There were fourteen members of the expedition and fourteen Norwegians in the crew. The members of the expedition were:

Gino Watkins—Leader
Jamie Scott—In charge of dogs
Ted Bingham—Doctor
Percy Lemon—Signal Officer
Jimmy D'Aeth—Pilot
Iliffe Cozens—Pilot and Photographer
Wilfred Hampton—Aircraft Maintenance
Laurence Wager—Geologist

Quintin Riley—Meteorologist
Alfred Stephenson—Chief Surveyor
John Rymill—Surveyor
Martin Lindsay—Surveyor
Freddy Chapman—Ornithologist
Augustine Courtauld—Surveyor and in charge of boats.

After coaling at Reykjavik we sailed for the ice. This gave us the chance to get some seals, for our dogs as well as ourselves. We hung up the seal-meat in the rigging to dry so that it could be kept for future dog food. When we were held up, we played games on the ice. John Rymill used to take off all his clothes and go on the ice to crack his forty-foot stock whip; a most impressive performance.

We got through the pack in the latitude of Cape Dan and put in to the Eskimo settlement of Angmagssalik. It was splendid to see the natives coming out in their kayaks to meet us, throwing their harpoons. At Angmagssalik we picked up an Eskimo pilot to help us find a place for our Base. We found a fjord about thirty miles from the settlement; at its head was a glacier which came down from the ice cap. Unlike most of the Greenland glaciers, this one looked as though it were possible to sledge up it. On the other side of the fjord from the glacier was a low point of land where we decided to build our house. The local Eskimos seemed to be very much against this, but since at that time we could not understand them, we took no notice. Later, when the wind came, we found out how right they were.

These were Gino's plans:

1. To map the coast both North and South of our base for some hundreds of miles, so that future aircraft be able to find out where they were.
2. To make a record of the weather at our base.
3. To maintain a weather station on the summit of the ice cap

throughout the year. (No-one had ever been on the ice cap in winter before, so no-one knew what happened there).

The first thing to do was to unload the ship and start building our house. In this the crew of the *Quest* helped us a lot. All night we worked in the hold shovelling coal, while in the daytime the ship's carpenter and some of the hands started on the house. Unfortunately, we were trying out a wind-generator with a large metal propeller. This was on the bridge, and one day the carpenter, wanting to see what it was like, stuck his finger into the propeller; it was cut off.

There was also the job of putting up the two seventy-foot wireless masts. For this we had to make holes in the rock to support the stays. The rock was very hard.

At last the house was finished and secured to the ground with wire hawsers over the roof. All the stores had been landed; some of them, especially the wireless gear, were very heavy. The Met. station was also put up, and now some of us could sail in the *Quest* up the coast to start our survey work. We took our Moths, which by now had been assembled on floats, in order to get air-photographs. On our way up the coast, the geologist and the surveyors used to go ashore in one of the ship's boats with an outboard motor. It was not easy to find a safe place to leave the boat, especially as there were no tide tables. One morning we found the boat hanging vertically by its painter; the oars were lost and we made our way back to the ship paddling with the floor boards.

I took the astronomical observations while Alfred Stephenson did the plane tabling. Laurence Wager used to go off with his rucksack and hammer to collect specimens of the rocks. Whenever ice conditions allowed, the Moth was used for taking photographs from ten thousand feet; these helped in the map-making.

Eventually we reached the great fjord of Kangerdlugsuak. This fjord had never been entered by a white man, nor was it inhabited by Eskimos. We penetrated about forty miles towards its head. Here we found an enormous glacier coming down; it had a floating tongue about a mile long and two miles across. We set about surveying the fjord with our boat. Great mountains rose up along the sides in sharp peaks about seven thousand feet high. In our survey work we had difficulty in finding anywhere to camp, the sides of the fjord being so steep. There was a lot of wild life, and once we came close to a mother bear and her cub. She swam with it to an ice floe, heaved herself out of the water on to the ice and started loping away. The cub, however, could not manage to scramble up, and soon the mother returned and hauled it on to the floe by the scruff of its neck.

While we were away mapping, Jimmy D'Aeth and Gino in the Moth were busy taking photographs. One day Gino spotted a big range of mountains far inland. It is probable that this was the famous Hvitserk, the seamark of the Vikings. These mountains cannot be seen from the coast but only from far out at sea. Five years later, some of us climbed this range and found the highest peak to be 12,200 feet. The Danes named them "The Watkins Mountains".

When we returned to the base, Jamie and a party were away setting up the ice cap station.

Percy Lemon was in charge of the base and was maintaining contact by wireless with Angmagssalik. The links which he had arranged in England with various amateurs and Royal Signal officers had been ruled out by the GPO. He had installed two Eskimo girls to look after us. They slept in the loft and their wages were two cigarettes a day and permission to play the gramophone. There was one tune they were very fond of. We got sick of it and threw the record out of the window. It smashed to pieces on the stones, but the girls, nothing daunted, sewed it up with sealskin thread and the wretched thing went on playing again!

10

Gino's Expedition

Ice Cap

WHEN GINO returned to the base, he told us he had set up the ice cap station about one hundred and thirty miles to the NW, at a height of about eight thousand feet, and that he had marked the route with a flag, every half mile. Besides finding the astronomical position of the station, he had made a route book in which the compass bearing of each flag from the next one was noted. Quintin Riley and Martin Lindsay were the first occupants, and the plan was that the station should be relieved every four to six weeks.

The next job was to make a dump of the sledging stores for the second relief journey. The bottom part of the glacier was too difficult to get up, so we had to ferry the stores across the fjord and then carry them on our backs up the steep rocks to the glacier. We thought we could get the Eskimos to help with this work, but they soon became bored and we had to do it ourselves. I spent quite a time at the foot of the cliffs getting the pemmican out of its tins and into linen bags, to save weight.

We started for the ice cap station at the end of October. There were five of us on this trip: Freddy Chapman, in charge of the party, Percy Lemon, to install the wireless we were taking to the station, Laurence Wager, "Steve" (Alfred Stephenson) and myself. We had five sledges, one of which carried the wireless.

A gale of wind came up while we were camped on the bare ice of the glacier, and various things were blown over the edge, but we managed to save our tents. The dogs had to wear canvas boots until we got the sledges to the snow. Unfortunately we were short of these, since somebody had ordered fifty pairs of boots for fifty dogs.

The next difficulty was Bug Bear Bank. The united strength of dogs and men was not enough to get the sledges up this steep hill on the glacier. We therefore drove steel pitons into the ice and hauled the sledges up by block and tackle. Owing to the length of the tackle, we could only haul a sledge a short distance at a time; it took several days before we had everything at the top: After this, for about ten miles, there was an area of crevasses. It was impossible to see these, as they were completely covered by snow, and at any moment a whole team might be engulfed. When this happened, we hauled the dogs out by their traces. We used to have a man walking in front prodding the snow with an ice-axe. Finding a way through the crevasses took several days.

Then we struck the gales. Before we left the base our first "fornicator" had hit us. I was doing the weather recordings at the time and crawled out to get the force of the wind from the anemometer. The instrument registered 129 mph before it blew away. It was lucky our hut had been wired to the ground. Boxes and gear flew about, and one could only go outdoors on hands and knees. Now, on the ice cap, these winds caused a high drift of snow which the dogs could not face; moreover, they swept the surface into ridges like waves of the sea, with hard tops and soft hollows. As a result the sledges were constantly overturning, so that they got broken and we had to spend a lot of time mending them. This was not too easy, for we had to take our gloves off to tie the knots.

The tents were a marvel. They had been designed by Gino and were pyramid-shaped, depending on four bamboos over which the outer cover was spread. There was a thin inner covering suspended by tapes from the bamboos. Each tent had a wide skirt on which we used to put the ration boxes and plenty of snow; this kept it down. You entered by a round opening in one side, which fastened with tape. However fierce the wind, these tents never blew away. We had reindeer skins on the floor and lived in down sleeping bags. The dogs would curl up in their harnesses in the snow outside and seemed quite happy. We had to be careful about putting inside the tent everything the dogs could eat: gloves, aluminium cooking pots and even binoculars were liable to disappear.

After about a fortnight, we had covered very little of our journey. We met Gino, returning with Jamie from a sledge trip, but he could do little to help us. He said we must decide what to do according to the conditions. It was clear that it would take a long time to get to the ice cap station, but we had to relieve the two men who were there and would soon be running out of food. In order to take on the maximum amount of provisions, we sent back two men with Gino, abandoned the wireless sledge (it was never seen again) and took on all their food.

The rations were made up into boxes. Each box was supposed to supply two men for a week, but we found that at that height we did not need to eat so much and could make a box last twelve days. The dogs were fed on a pound of pemmican and a quarter pound of fat once a day. This diet tended to give them diarrhoea, but otherwise they seemed to do pretty well on it.

Our rations had been planned by Gino. He had little to go on, since the last wintering expedition in the Arctic had been that of Nares in 1875. However, he had learnt a lot from the mistakes made in the Antarctic and had consulted the best authorities in England. One extremely valuable part of our rations was concentrated lemon juice. Captain Cook had discovered that this was a preventative of scurvy, but unfortunately the Admiralty and the Merchant Service found lime juice was cheaper. This had not nearly the same amount of Vitamin C, and sailors, as well as members of Polar expeditions, continued to die of this terrible disease. Gino had got together with an expert who, after many experiments on rats, had produced for the first time a concentrated form of lemon juice—an antiscorbutic it was possible to take on a sledge journey.

It would be wearisome to say much more about this long-drawn out journey. For days we had to lie in our tents listening to the roar of the wind. Travel was out of the question; even when we went out of the tent to feed the dogs, it was difficult to find the way back. I shared a tent with Freddy. We each had one small book and he used to read to me out of *The Golden Treasury*. When movement was possible, we would sometimes only do a mile in a day's journey. We were driving on the fan method, where each dog is on a separate trace. The trouble was that the dogs kept jumping over each other's traces until the whole lot got into a solid, frozen tangle. We would then have to spend a long time, working clumsily in our gloves, to straighten them out. One day on the trail a bitch in my team, who was pulling well, produced a litter of pups. These were promptly gobbled up by the rest of the team. She carried on pulling.

At last the storms died down and it was clear, cold weather. It was 40° below zero, and we had some difficulty in finding the flags, which were snowed up. We dared not miss one in case we lost the way altogether; there were no landmarks whatever. After six weeks we arrived. The inmates were thankful to see us—we were, of course, long overdue. Clearly we could not count on relieving the station during the winter and it was already the beginning of December. And it seemed a great pity to abandon the place after all the effort that had been put into setting it up.

I worked it out that, with the little food we had brought, I could last out alone for five months. As I had frostbite in my toes, I had no wish to make the journey back. So I decided to stay on my own and keep the station going. We had a great Christmas dinner in advance; then I said good-bye to my companions and, on December 5th, they left. There were some books which had been brought up by the first people. Among them was the Bible, *Great Sea Stories of All Nations, Vanity Fair, Guy Mannering, Jane Eyre, The Forsyte Saga, Kidnapped, The Master of Ballantrae* and *Whitaker's Almanack*.

Every four hours I had to go out to read the weather instruments. The station consisted of a dome-shaped tent, eight feet in diameter, and a snow house built over the top of it. It was entered by a tunnel which came up through the floor, on the igloo principle. Ventilation was provided by a two-inch pipe at the top. There were also two small snow houses, reached through branches off the main tunnel; these were used for stores. The whole thing was surrounded by a snow wall. This proved to be rather a mistake. Whenever there was wind, both the inside of the enclosure and the entrance to the tunnel got drifted up, and I found that, owing to the pain in my toes, I could not stay out long enough to dig all the drift away.

Inside the house, I kept very warm. I lay in a reindeer-skin sleeping bag and, in addition to the Primus stove I used for cooking, there was an Aladdin lamp which gave out a good heat.

After a little while, I noticed a lot of itching on my arms. When I took off my vest I found a number of lice. I remembered then that I had lent my sleeping bag to one of the Eskimo girls at the base. I put my clothes outside for a couple of days to kill off the creatures, but when I dressed again I found the lice biting away as happily as ever. I then put out the clothes for a fortnight in about 50° below zero. This seemed to do them in.

Outside, when the wind wasn't blowing, it was amazingly still. The only thing you could hear was the blood pounding in your ears. Far in the sky, the Northern Lights waved and shimmered. At times they looked like waving curtains; at others like the beams of hidden searchlights. All around it was utterly flat; in every direction snow stretched to the horizon like the sea. There was no life on the ice cap. I never saw a bird, or even a fly.

As time went on, I began to keep a look-out for the Moth. Jimmy D'Aeth, whom I relieved, had promised to fly up and drop me some good things and some news. I found out afterwards that although they had started several times with the Moth on skis, they could never find the station. Later, both the Moths were damaged. One went into the tide crack, and the other was tethered out on the ice when a gale came on. A gang of Eskimos was roped in to hold it down, but when a sudden gust came, they were so frightened it was going to fly away with them that they all let go. The plane was blown over and smashed. Both Moths, however, were eventually repaired with shirt cloth and driftwood.

One day in February a strange thing happened. I was lying in my sleeping bag when suddenly I heard a noise like an underground train coming. The noise ended in a mighty crash. I thought at first that the whole station might have dropped into a crevasse; however, everything seemed to be all right. When I had got over it sufficiently, I ventured out to see what had happened. To my amazement, everything looked exactly as before. The Union Jack was quietly waving in the wind; the snow all round was just as level as it always had been. Scientists now think this must have been a snow-quake.

By March, with the increasing daylight, I thought the relief party might come. In fact, a sledge party under Jamie Scott did set out with this purpose, but the route flags were snowed up and invisible, and since they had not a time-signal set with them, they were not able to find their longitude accurately. Eventually they got into a six day blizzard and had to lie up. Rather than go on searching blindly, Jamie decided to go back to the base while his dogs were still fit, so that a better equipped expedition could set out.

The tunnel entrance finally got so blocked with drift, that I could no longer get out by it. I then made a hole in the roof of one of the small snow houses and closed it with a ration box, filling up the cracks all round with snow. For some weeks this worked very well. But one day, when it was blowing hard, I found the snow house full of fine drift coming in like high pressure steam through a little hole under the box. It was impossible to get out this way, as the only place to put the snow was in the tunnel behind me, and this would have cut me off from the house. I then made a hole in the roof of the other snow house, but the shaft up to the surface was too long. After a day or two, so much snow came down the shaft on top of the box, that I could no longer move it. I was then imprisoned.

Naturally, I worked out all the possible things that could have happened to prevent them coming for me. It occurred to me that there might have been an epidemic of distemper among the dogs, or that the base might have caught fire and all the harnesses been destroyed. Yet as time went on, I began to feel complete confidence. I knew that, even if Gino was having to wait for better weather, he wouldn't let me down. I began to realize that I should not be left to die. I came to know that I was held by the Everlasting Arms.

One of my last sallies into the outside world was to dig up my last remaining four-gallon tin of paraffin and the last of my ration boxes—not easy to find, as they were hidden under six feet of snow. When I got out the paraffin tin, I discovered it was empty; it must have been damaged in the journey up. After a time, light and fuel gave out, and so did tobacco. I then smoked tea. One trouble in these days was the bulging-in of the walls due to the weight of snow on the roof. Another was the formation of ice inside the house. There was a certain amount in my sleeping-bag, caused by condensation, which meant I had to lie with my feet curled up. When the light failed, I used to amuse myself by singing—mostly the *Beggar's Opera* or Gilbert and Sullivan. It was an awful row, but there was no one to hear it. I had a shot at making a lamp with a tin of ski-wax and a piece of string for a wick, but it wasn't much good.

During April there was another snow-quake. This time I couldn't get out to see what had happened, but no doubt if I had, there would have been nothing visible, as before.

I kept a little paraffin so that I could make myself some porridge every morning. On May 5th, exactly five months since I was left here, and on the day I had told Gino the rations would run out, the Primus gave its last gasp. Very soon there was a noise like a football match overhead. They had come!

A hole of brilliant daylight appeared in the roof. There was Gino's face and Gino's voice saying, "Put these on." He handed me a pair of snow-glasses. How different it was from the last time I had seen the outside world! It was May now and dazzling sunshine; I had not realized it would be like this. They lost no time in pulling me out and I found I was quite all right. My legs were a bit weak, but I managed to make my way slowly under my own steam to their camp about a mile and a half away. Freddy Chapman and John Rymill were with Gino. They had had a quick journey from the base, starting out as soon as Jamie got back. The weather on the ice cap was now good.

Before leaving the station, we dismantled the weather instruments. The minimum thermometer had been down to sixty-four below zero (96° of frost).

We set out for home the next day. I rode on a sledge the whole way, reading *The Count of Monte Cristo*. Conditions were good and we completed the journey in five days; it had taken us six weeks on the way up. One day a large aeroplane came over and showered us with boxes of food. It was the Swedish airman Ahrenberg, who had flown out from Sweden to look for the ice cap station.

With the dogs pulling like mad, we rushed down to the fjord. It was, of course, frozen hard, and we soon sledged across to the base. At four a.m. we walked in and woke them up. It was a great reception. I remember an Eskimo woman coming out of the hut to welcome me. I could not understand a word she said, but she kissed me, which was explicit enough.

Perhaps it is worth putting on record that, besides bringing along the snow-glasses for me, Gino had provided himself with a prayer book. This was just like him; he had a genius for thinking everything out.

Hanging up in our hut we had a piece of polished wood painted with a verse by Masefield. It was presented to the expedition by Admiral Sir William Goodenough, President of the Royal Geographical Society, and these were the lines on it:

> The Power of man is as his hopes.
> In darkest night, the cocks are crowing.
> With the sea roaring and the wind blowing;
> Adventure. Man the ropes.

John Riddoch Rymill, Henry George 'Gino' Watkins,
Augustine Courtauld, Frederick Spencer Chapman.

With Ejnar Mikkelsen (1880-1971), polar explorer and 1924 founder of Scoresbysund (now Ittoqqortoormiit) in Greenland, one of the most remote settlements on earth.

The Ice Cap Station, December 1930.

II

Gino's Expedition

The Boat Journey

I T WAS wonderful being back at the base among my companions again. We could go everywhere by sledge and we paid calls on our Eskimo friends. On Sundays we used to have a service in our hut, conducted by Quintin. He had a pirate hymn book and I remember how we sat on our bunks letting rip with one of the hymns which went to the tune of "Clementine"—

"Oh my darling, oh my darling, oh my DARLING
Clementine..."

At other times we would sing some of the Trappers' songs that Gino and Jamie brought back from Labrador: "Baby, lie easy", "Down among the Cornbrake", "Alleluia, I'm a bum", and many more.

When the ice broke up, the kayaking started. Gino was very keen to learn the Eskimo ways of hunting seals. Several of us got quite good at it, notably Gino himself and Freddy Chapman. They learnt to roll. This is a trick which you can use when you get upset, which very easily happens, especially when you are fast to a seal by the harpoon line. If you don't know how to do it you are left hanging upside down in the water. Since the kayak is built to fit you, it is generally impossible to get out under water, and if the seal is a bladder-nose, it will come and eat your face. It was arranged that a film should be taken of us all rolling together. I made a mess of my roll and got stuck under water, but luckily I am of slim build and managed to wriggle out and swim to the surface.

Doc and I went to another fjord by boat to do some mapping. This was, perhaps the most pleasant time of the whole expedition. He used to catch fish (Arctic char) in the stream, while I climbed the hills with my plane table. The weather was perfect and cooking Doc's "salmon" in the frying pan at night was great fun.

As another contribution to the mapping, John Rymill and I set out in one of our whale-boats to make a survey of the coast south of the base, but it proved to be too early in the year for boat travel. After a week trying to get through the ice, we returned with only one point fixed for our map.

One day at the base, Gino asked, "I say, August, would you like to come with me on the boat journey?" Now, I had heard about this boat journey and had decided that nothing would induce me to go. For one thing, I thought our whale-boats could never make the six hundred miles to Julianahaab on the west coast. For another, I was supposed to be getting married when I got home and knew my young woman was waiting for me. But no-one could resist Gino and of course I said "Yes". Gino never gave orders, he just asked you to do something. You always did it.

We took our whale-boat to Angmagssalik to be fitted out by an Eskimo carpenter. It was splendid seeing our friends again. There was the Danish Governor, who was also the storekeeper, the wireless operator, who sent all our telegrams, and Pastor Rosing, a Greenlander from the west coast. Rosing was something of an artist and had painted a picture of Ahrenberg climbing with his great Junkers flying boat from the water on to an ice floe.

So that we could keep our stores dry, we had the bows of our boat decked in, and we also had a mast stepped to enable us to sail when our outboard engine broke down.

The previous summer when I had been at the settlement, we had had a signal that a man had been hurt in the engine room of the Danish ship. There was no doctor at the settlement, so Doc and I went round in our whale-boat to see if we could help. We travelled all night, during which Doc gave me instructions on giving an anaesthetic. When we reached the ship, it was found that an operation was unnecessary. This was just as well, as Doc told me afterwards that he couldn't stand the sight of blood.

The supply ship soon arrived and came round to our base to embark our stores and the party for home. This consisted of the whole expedition except John Rymill and Wilfred Hampton, who planned to sledge across the ice cap to the west coast; Jamie Scott, Martin and Steve, who were to sledge south-west to Ivigtut; and the boat party—Gino, Percy Lemon and myself. All three parties set off in August. John and "Ham" carried kayaks on their sledges, as they had a long fjord to get down on the other side. The kayaks had to be raised on specially built frames so that they would not be eaten by the dogs. I had made a signal home for suet to be sent by the supply ship—I got a suit!

When we of the boat party set out, we took two whale-boats, one towing the other, and our three kayaks. These whale-boats had been part of the equipment of the *Quest*. They were carvel-built and very strong.

Since we could not carry sufficient petrol for the journey, Gino had persuaded Nicodemus (the father of our local Eskimo family) to help us by taking his family to winter at Umivik fjord, about one hundred and fifty miles south of the base. There was a slight difficulty about this because Nicodemus said he could not take his own umiak (the women's boat); the skins were too old. He said, however, that he could get another one from a settlement about forty miles away, so we took him there and in five minutes he had swapped his old umiak for another one. We then set out for the base, towing him and his family in their new ship. He had brought his wife and his girls to row (the men never row the umiak). After a bit, Nicodemus said there was something wrong with it; the umiak would not steer and he thought the keel must be warped. So back we went to Kulusuk, where he swapped it for another one.

Again we set out, but going through the ice, the umiak grazed a floe. Suddenly there was great commotion. It seemed the ice had made a long tear in the skin, and the boat was quickly filling with water. We towed her alongside the floe and everyone got out in a hurry. They soon had the umiak out on the ice. In ten minutes Nicodemus's wife had sewn up the rent and all was well again. They went off in their umiak three weeks before us, carrying, as the custom is, all their children, dogs and possessions. He took his wife, his son, his four daughters, his grand-daughter, one child of eight years old that his son-in-law had lent him, two sledges, ten dogs, his tent and a year's supplies. In addition to this, he took twenty-seven gallons of petrol for us.

This coast had only been traversed once before, a hundred years earlier, by a naval officer, Lieutenant Graah, sent out by the King of Denmark. He had made the voyage in the reverse direction in an Eskimo umiak rowed by women. The main object of our trip, apart from mapping the coast, was to see if we could live off the country by the Eskimo methods of hunting.

All went well for the first week, when we had fine weather, but after this we got held up at the island of Pikiuti for several days. A week or two later we reached Umivik. We used to camp wherever we could find a place for the boats. One trouble, we found, was the mosquitoes. Whenever we went ashore, they would rise in a dense cloud and attack us. As there were no other living creatures on this coast, they were out for our blood. So thick were they that we could not take a photo.

Gino used to do the hunting with his white painted kayak, Percy Lemon the survey, and I the cooking, the boatwork and the astronomical observations, as well as giving a hand with the mapping. One day I made a wonderful pudding of suet and boubukas, a kind of bilberry which grows on the hillsides. These are gathered by the girls in the autumn and are the only vegetable food the Eskimos get the whole year round.

Nicodemus was very pleased with the great fjord of Umivik. He found there more seals than he had ever seen in his life. It used to be a wintering place in the old days, but since the establishment of the store at Angmagssalik, the Eskimo families did not care to go that distance.

We said good-bye to Nicodemus and his family and proceeded on our way down the coast. Soon the pack ice, which had protected us from the sea, died out. We were left exposed to the Atlantic. One day it came on to blow onshore. The map wasn't much help, but we sighted a fjord not far away; the trouble was that its entrance was defended by a line of icebergs. I was steering the leading boat and just as we were beginning to get through the bergs, it began to roll badly and fill with water. Percy Lemon jumped aboard to help bale. He threw overboard the seal meat I was carrying. Then the engine conked out and jumped over the stern; I retrieved it just in time. We took to the oars, got through a narrow passage between the bergs, and found a little cove where we beached the boats. "Thank God," we said.

We spent some days at this place. On each of them we went up the nearby hill to have a look at the state of the ice, but always it was too bad for our boats. Once we thought we heard a motor boat far away. Gino dashed up the hill to light a bonfire, but could see nothing. We heard afterwards that Dr. Knud Rassmussen had passed down the coast. He had been driven far out into the pack and had lost his rudder.

One night the spring tide came. While we were asleep in our tent, our boat was floated off the beach, turned round and upset. Most of our stores, including the oatmeal, got wet.

The next snag was the famous glacier of Puisortok. This, the Eskimos had told us, was so dangerous that it could not be passed. They said that ice from it went like a torpedo under the water, to come up and sink you far out to sea. Also we were told that we must make no noise, or even speak, until we had passed it.

When we came to this place, we saw a mass of brash ice, in small pieces like porridge, stretching a long way. We had to wait some days before the weather was fit to let us go round it, for we had an experience new to us in Greenland: it rained. One night our little tent got flooded, and Gino found himself sleeping in water. More serious than this, and something which depressed him very much, was the fact that the skins on the kayaks were going rotten with the continual wet. Also new ice was starting to form.

But at last there came a fine day and, by going out several miles to sea, we got past Puisortok. The front of the glacier extended for about thirty miles. We used to fill up the petrol tank from a teapot while the boat was under way; this saved stopping the engine and so getting caught in the ice.

We had now only one boat, having abandoned the second as the amount of stores was reduced. Among other things, tobacco had started to run out. Gino didn't smoke, but Percy announced that without cigarettes, he would certainly go mad and probably murder one of us. I lent him a pipe, which kept him happy until pipe tobacco was finished too. Percy remained quite happy, though he said that if anyone had told him he could survive without smoking, he would never have believed him. We left behind in the second boat the useless wireless set and some other gear, including a beautiful Class A chronometer.

At one point we were completely held up by our engine refusing to work. Percy Lemon, who was our engineer, said he would take it to pieces but that it would take him a fortnight to make the tools. While he was asleep ashore, utterly exhausted by struggling with the engine, I thought I would have a go. I found a screw on it which I had never noticed before and took this out. Immediately the engine started with a roar. Percy Lemon, hearing it, came out of his tent in amazement. We left our fjord in a glorious sunrise.

Our next headache was the boat herself, which had become very leaky. One of us had to sleep on board every night so as to bale her out every few hours. When we could not find a place to beach her, we used to lay out an anchor and haul her out by a block attached to the anchor ring. One night while we had her moored in a little cove under the lee of an island, the stern warp chafed through, so that the boat got badly bumped on the rocks. Percy made a splendid job of repairing her with pieces of wood cut from the floorboards; nevertheless, the water still came in.

There were no people living on this coast, but eventually we found a fjord where there were three Norwegians. They had come to hunt foxes and bears but were not having much luck; the hunting was bad and they had no kayaks for the seals. They were, however, great experts on boats and soon had ours hauled out for repairs. They poured water inside, which gushed forth in a dozen places, but Mortinsen, the chief hunter, soon got it fixed for us.

We now travelled flat out, going for twenty-four hours whenever it was possible. At last we came to Prince Christian Sound, which cuts off Cape Farewell and the toe of Greenland. It was now the October of 1931, and the new ice was forming rapidly. We had difficulty in forcing our way through it.

We got to the first settlement. Here Gino had laid on some petrol for us. Unfortunately, "petrol" in Danish means "paraffin"! We hoped the engine would not notice the difference of a half-and-half mixture— but it did. We ended our journey with one gallon of petrol left.

Gino stepped ashore at Nanortalik and said, *"God Dag!"* Knud Rassmussen was there to meet us. So ended Gino's last journey. If the expedition had boasted a motto, it might well have been Gino's own: *Carpe Diem*—Seize the Day. He was killed the next year while hunting in his kayak alone.

We found when we arrived that nothing had been heard of John and Ham, so Gino and I went up the west coast in a motor boat with a Greenlander for pilot. Some times his sweater got into the engine, which didn't help. At length we got to Holsteinsborg, where John and Ham were supposed to have arrived, and after we had waited a few days, they turned up, annoyed that we had come to look for them. We sailed home together in the Danish four-masted schooner *Hans Egede*.

In Copenhagen we had a great reception, with National Anthems and speeches. Jamie Scott, Quintin, Pam Watkins (Gino's sister) and Nannie Watkins were there to meet us.

During the boat journey, Gino had planned an expedition round the Arctic, but when he got back to England, he was persuaded to abandon his plans and go off to the Antarctic to make a journey across the continent, as Bunny Fuchs is doing now. However, after a lot of time and trouble, he could not raise sufficient money for this expedition and was eventually won over to going back to Greenland to carry on the same work. With three other men, he went to Lake Fjord, where he met his death.

There are one or two things about this truly remarkable man which ought to be mentioned. One was his attitude to the Eskimos: he thought they were better people than we were, and I think he was right. What he wanted to do above all was to study their hunting methods and way of life. Another thing was his attitude towards people: he once told me he did not mind a bit how bad a temper a man had so long as he was efficient.

We once had a discussion on how you felt when you were tired. Gino said he had never been tired in his life, as he had never taken sufficient exercise. This rather put an end to the argument. When we were sledging he would sleep in a single down sleeping-bag, while most of us were feeling chilly in a double one, or reindeer-skin bags.

There is much more, of course, that I could say about Gino, but I don't propose to do it. Jamie Scott put all he could of him into that brave book, *Gino Watkins*; and Jamie is a writer besides being Gino's friend.

Henry George 'Gino' Watkins (1907-1932).

12

Mollie

MOLLIE MONTGOMERIE was the daughter of Frank Douglas Montgomerie and Esme Napier, both splendid people coming of a fine line. She was a descendant of the "Fighting Napiers" from the time of Nelson and Wellington. We had known each other, as boy and girl, for many years.

Mollie was very musical and had a lovely voice. She used to learn singing with old Yarrow, and belonged to the London Philharmonic Choir. I used to go to her choir rehearsals—*The Dream of Gerontius* or Bach's St. Matthew "Passion"—which I very much enjoyed. Later, she persuaded me to learn with Yarrow too. I've never had much of a voice, but Yarrow was a charming teacher and I used to like trying to sing the songs of Herrick. At that time, the *Beggar's Opera* was popular, and Mollie and I used to sing the duets from it—without an audience, luckily. I never forgot those old songs, and that is how I came to be singing them to keep myself company on the ice cap.

In 1928 I decided to see how Mollie—tall, slender and very pretty—would take to the kind of life I liked. At that time I was sailing partner with Frank Carr in his fine old pilot cutter *Cariad*. He and I sailed her to the west coast of Scotland, via Ireland, and there Mollie joined us with her chaperon Avis Hodgson, who later married the Reverend F. Spurway. *Cariad* was still as she was built in 1904. There were no sheets, only somewhat smelly blankets. In order to save water, I used to inspect the basin every morning after the girls had washed; if the water was clean enough to serve another turn, they were made to use it again. The men, of course, just didn't wash.

The Bos'n, a Naval Pensioner, was our paid hand and also did the cooking. With luck, we used to get lunch about four p.m. We had a glorious time sailing about the islands, although the Bos'n was rather inclined to let things go so that they fell on our heads. *Cariad*'s gear was heavy.

When we got back from the trip, so far as I was concerned, Mollie had passed the test. Seeing her off at the station at Aberdeen I asked her to marry me. It did not go down too well.

Mollie Montgomerie on Cariad.

I then left on Wordie's Petermann expedition. When I got back, I tried again, twice, with more success the third time. We became engaged. The following year I went off to Greenland with Gino Watkins.

When Jamie Scott returned from the ice cap without finding the station, Gino felt that he must tell the world in case of further trouble. He therefore made a signal to *The Times*, which had our press rights. This found my father, mother and Betty in mid-Atlantic, returning from my father's one and only visit to the States. A lot of signalling ensued. Aeroplanes and ice breakers set out to the rescue. Luckily only one plane got through, and that was Ahrenberg's. When the fuss started in the press, Mollie was in Salzburg with my old friends Francis and Mary Rodd; they were listening to the lovely music of Mozart in the open air. Later, when the news of the relief came through, Mollie was at home at Great Codham Hall, Essex. She was, of course, invaded by the minions of the press, who explained that if they went back to their papers without a story, they would get the sack. Mollie, with her soft heart, had to think something up.

She had a bit of a shock again when I signalled that I should not be returning with the rest of the expedition but was going on the boat journey with Gino. Luckily, we did not have to winter again and got back to Copenhagen in November.

Mollie's parents had now left Codham. Her father, who was a great expert on old oak, bought an old barn which he transported piece by piece, on the back of a disused Ford, to build a house at the little hamlet of Rotten End. As there was no home ready for her to be married from, Mollie and I decided to get it done at Southwark Cathedral. The wedding was on a Saturday, January 2nd, 1932.

The night before, I gave a small bachelor party at the Café Royal. We then descended on the Fun Fair at Olympia. Taffy Rodd and I got into a "Dodgem" motorboat on a pond. We sank. When we had got ashore, a bit of trouble started with some large men in white sweaters. This was eventually stopped by Francis Rodd, who advanced on the mêlée in his evening cloak. I finished the evening with a black eye which my best man, Guy Wreford-Brown, treated with raw steak for the rest of the night. The next day was quite a "do": all our friends, my father's tenants and the family turned up.

We went for our wedding trip to the Sudan, where we stayed with my old friend Charles de Bunsen. We trekked with him round his district by camel, which was most enjoyable, and we saw something of the Arabs as well as taking a trip to the south, where the naked Nubas put on a war dance for us. One day when we were on trek, Mollie said to me, "What are you thinking about?" I replied, "Relativity."

On the return journey we stayed at Venice with Mollie's uncle, Alan Napier, who was British Consul there. We had a splendid time gondoling about the canals.

Mollie and August Courtauld in Venice, 1932.

When we got back we took a house in Trafalgar Square (now Chelsea Square) in Chelsea. I used to do revolver practice in my little writing room, pinning the target to telephone books to save the wall. Unfortunately, the telephone books tended to fall down at the critical moment. My shooting didn't do the wall any good.

At this house our first child, Perina, was born in December.

In addition to the Chelsea house, we took an old farmhouse by the sea, near Tichfield. It has a lovely rose garden and was near the Hamble river. In the summertime we used to go down there and I sailed *Duet* round from Burnham to berth her in the Hamble. Sometimes we would go out to watch the great yachts racing in the Solent, and occasionally we would sail to the lovely Beaulieu river or up Southampton Water.

Mollie became a first-rate helmsman, and often she would be left alone in the cockpit while the rest of us were for'ard dealing with the anchor, moorings or the sails. At the start of races she used to look after the stop watch and give me, every five seconds, the time left before the gun. When things were tricky in a race, turning to windward in a light air, for instance, it was she I used to put at the helm.

In September 1934 our second child was born—a boy, Christopher. He arrived in the middle of the night, and I remember going out into the street to dance with my mother-in-law.

By this time we had another house in Chelsea—18 Tite Street. The only trouble with this house was that it was inhabited by crickets, which used to set up an awful din. By squinting into a little hole under the stairs, I could see the chief offender. I tried firing my revolver at him, but it didn't seem to make much difference.

About this period, Mollie started to help me with a certain plan of mine. British ships were sinking all over the place, for no apparent reason, and we thought something ought to be done about it. I found out some of the facts of the situation, and it seemed to me that things were very bad indeed. I got together with Captain Coombs, a wonderful man, who gave me more information that supported what I had in mind. I then tried various MPs, who said they could do nothing; Lloyds, who said that they only did Insurance business and had no power to help; and finally I wrote a letter to *The Times*. This was returned with a note from the Editor saying that to publish it would be most unfair on British shipping. I got an introduction to the Under Secretary of the Board of Trade: he talked for half an hour about boating and then I was bowed out. I went to see the Head Official of the Safety of Ships Department in the Board of Trade: I had about two hours with him, and he frankly admitted that he was most disturbed about the situation. As a private person I could do no more—I am told that things are much better now.

The following year I thought I would get up an expedition to have a stab at the mountains Gino had discovered. I thought it would be nice for Mollie to see Greenland, so I asked the married men to bring their wives. It was, of course, quite unheard of for women to go on an Arctic expedition, and everyone said it was bound to be an appalling failure. Two of the wives were to winter with Laurence Wager's party, which was staying on to do geological work. Mollie had to have her appendix out just before we sailed, but was fit in the nick of time to come up to Aberdeen and join the *Quest*. The four girls survived all right and I think they enjoyed it; they certainly made themselves very useful.

At length we decided it was no good living in London any longer. Chelsea was constantly in a rain of soot, and the only place to take the children out was Battersea Park, a dismal piece of ground. Our summer abode, Brownwich (pronounced "Brinith") was also rapidly becoming impossible. For one thing, there was the smell of the new oil refinery at Fawley, and for another, the unceasing noise of the aeroplanes. So we made up our minds to have one house only and moved back to the old family haunts in Essex. We bought the Georgian house of Spencer Grange—we call it Spencers—at Great Yeldham. This is still our home.

Mollie and August after his return from Greenland.

13

The Watkins Mountains

I HAVE MENTIONED already how, in 1934, some of us thought it would be a good idea to try to climb the Watkins Mountains, but the story of this Greenland expedition remains to be told.

To get into training for our climb, Ebbe Munck, Laurence Wager and I set off for Skye at Christmas-time in an open Lagonda. Munck was an old friend of mine; later he organized Danish Resistance in World War II. Apart from the mountaineering, Wager wanted to spend a winter continuing his geology on the Greenland coast.

We stayed at a house in Glen Brittle on Skye and spent every day learning climbing on the Cuillins under Wager's tuition. He had been with Ruttledge's Everest expedition and had climbed to a height of 28,000 feet on the northern side of the mountain. Although the weather prevented us from seeing the Cuillins until we stepped on them, we learnt how to walk across a steep face by leaning outwards, and various other mysteries of the art of climbing. After finishing with the Cuillins, we had a try at Liathach and Ben Eigh before returning south.

In the summer of 1935 we sailed away once more for Greenland. Again we had the *Quest*, commanded by Captain Schjelderup. Laurence Wager's wintering party included two wives, and there were two also in our summer party. Mollie and I left our two little children with their Nannie at Brownwich. Another Everest man was with us besides Wager: Jack Longland.

Our plan was to sledge by manhauling from the head of Kangerdlugsuak fjord to the mountains. We had mapped out a route from air photographs.

It turned out to be a bad ice year. For weeks we lay in the pack, utterly stuck. Dynamite had no effect, and one day the Captain descended from the crow's nest and told me he could do nothing more. He said, too, that since there was danger we might drift onto an iceberg, we had better get our stores on to the ice. There were certainly a good many icebergs about; we could count forty from the deck. Bergs have an entirely different rate of drift from pack ice. They draw much more water and may well be over two hundred feet high. If the ship touches one of these bergs, the chances are that an avalanche of ice will come down, smashing in the decks and very likely sinking the ship. Six Norwegian sealers were lost in this way this summer.

We quickly broke open the hold to get our stores out. Everything we wanted, of course, was under tons of coal and the timber of Wager's winter house, but everyone, including the women, worked with a will. We soon had a pile of emergency rations, tents and sleeping bags on the ice alongside the ship. Meanwhile, the iceberg was coming nearer and nearer. We watched it anxiously but could do nothing about it. At the last moment the direction of our drift changed and we found ourselves going past it.

At long last we got through the pack and put in at Angmagssalik. Here we embarked Enoch and his family. They came aboard complete with wife, children and granny, and lived in the hold, on top of the coal. During the winter they were to hunt seals for Wager and his party.

The Eskimo women were very interested in Mollie. They spent a long time examining her long, fair hair and were disappointed to find that it did not contain the proper quantity of pets. Eventually they got it tied up on the top of her head, like their own. There was, too, a little Eskimo boy who was a great favourite. He spent his time throwing a toy harpoon or shooting arrows with a toy bow. Eigil Knuth, who was a sculptor, made some good busts of the Eskimos.

We then sailed for the north. After a time, the weather became so bad that we had to put in to Irminger Fjord, and the Captain announced that he did not think he could get us to Kangerdlugsuak. We made a hurried survey of the air photographs and came to the conclusion that we had better push on to the mountains from where we now were, since so much of the summer had already gone.

After landing Helge Larsen and Count Eigil Knuth to dig up Eskimo remains, we got our gear ashore and started up the glacier. We had one Nansen sledge, fitted with runners shod with German silver, to carry our load; we found this travelled well, hauled by five men on skis using harnesses similar to those of the Scott expedition. A supporting party accompanied us for the first week. The going was good for a few miles and then we came to a steep hill leading to a col between the mountains. After that there was a difficult ice-fall leading down to the great Nordenskiold glacier, which must be one of the biggest in Greenland. It winds almost level between the mountains and eventually comes out at Kangerdlugsuak. We hauled up the great glacier for several days until we found ourselves on the far side, right under the range itself. The height was now about five thousand feet, and it seemed we would have some seven thousand feet to climb.

Leaving our sledge at the bottom, we ascended the mountain on snow all the way, a strenuous but easy climb. At last we got to the top; there was no higher peak in sight. There we hoisted the Danish and English flags, took a round of angles with the theodolite, and built a cairn in which we placed a record of the climb. The view in the evening sun was magnificent. We camped that night on the snow below the summit. The readings of our aneroids and boiling-point thermometer made the height 12,300 feet. This is considered, I believe, the highest mountain in the Arctic, and it was a great satisfaction that it had been climbed by two of Gino's men and by a mixed party of Danes and Englishmen.

We made a quick journey back to the coast, our load being now light. After landing Laurence Wager's wintering party, his house and stores, we sailed for home. By now the ice had moved south and we had an easy passage.

Laurence Wager returned home the following year with his party all complete. He had made some long sledge journeys which enabled him to do some good geology to add to his work on Gino's expedition.

Members of the 1935 Greenland Expedition on Quest
(August Courtauld far left).

14

Duet

SINCE I had not much to do in my solitary session at the ice cap station, I designed a yacht. This was my idea of the boat I should like to have when I got married. She was to be sufficiently seaworthy to go anywhere, was to have room for my wife and one or two friends, and be of moderate draught. I made her a yawl, thinking this would be the best rig for handling in difficult conditions when short-handed.

After I got home, I scoured the country in search of my boat. I even went as far afield as Milford Haven. At last I found the yawl *Gaviota* on the beach at Burnham-on-Crouch. This boat was almost exactly the same as the one I had designed. Although she was English built, *Gaviota* had spent most of her life in Germany and was entirely unknown. She was for sale.

I changed her name to *Duet*. This had been the name of my first boat and I thought it appropriate as I was just going to get married.

She has proved, in the twenty-five years I have owned her, the perfect vessel. Built at a time when materials were at their best and designed by a genius—Linton Hope—she is exceptionally fast with a leading wind or in light airs. She has berths for six below and a central companion way which leaves the after cabin completely shut off, so that people do not come through it in wet oilskins on their way off watch.

We took on a hand to look after her. He was Jack Bedford—a first-class sailor, a fine swimmer and a good cook.

Our first trip was to the west coast of Scotland in the summer of 1932.[1] Mollie joined me in the Clyde and we had the idyllic cruise that you usually get among those islands before she had to leave.

I sailed homeward bound from Oban, west about. The only crew I could muster was my somewhat elderly father-in-law. All went well as far as the Mull of Kintyre. Then in the middle of the night it started to blow hard from the east. *Duet* was caught in her ball dress, as the old sailors used to say; we had everything set, even the jackyard topsail. But we soon got her snugged down and set a compass course down the Irish Sea. The next thing that happened was a gun to port. We could just make out the dim shape of a light-ship and knew then that we must have got inside the Irish Lights. A little further and we should have been on the sands. We discovered afterwards that the compass had been deflected by the iron boom gallows stowed in the engine room.

When we got to Penzance we heard the news of the death of Gino Watkins in Greenland. We flew the ensign at half mast.

The following year we raced to Heligoland. The Hitler Machine was just warming up; it was not very pleasant for the English.

In 1934 we raced first to Heligoland and then on to Copenhagen. A bit of a snag cropped up before we started. The day before the start of the race, we were trying out a new balloon staysail in the Crouch. We were not looking where we were going and ran ashore on the top of high water. The following day, in spite of digging at low water and towing with motor boats at high, we failed to get her off before the start of the race. We had the mortification of seeing all our rivals sail past us while we were still hard and fast aground. A few hours later, on the top of the next tide, having unloaded our ballast, cable and stores, we got her off to make sail in chase, caught up most of our rivals in the North Sea and got a prize.

---

[1] Those with a special interest in sailing will find a record of the passages of *Duet* at the end of this book. ("Passages of *Duet*.")

A day or two after finishing at Heligoland—and after a collision with one of our competitors who rammed us on the counter in a race round the island—we started the race to Copenhagen. One of our competitors was an old English yacht manned by German submarine officers with orders from Hitler to win. She was considerably larger than the maximum limit allowed.

Another rival was the famous old *Thalassa*. She was manned by her owner, an aged Colonel, his butler and chauffeur. As we passed them, they asked us for the weather forecast, which we had just had from the BBC; it had mentioned easterly winds. They thereupon sailed as hard as they could inshore. Soon afterwards we got the Danish forecast, which was translated by Ebbe Munck. This said there would be a cooling" from the north-west. There certainly was. The Colonel in the *Thalassa* was hove-to for the next two days on a lee shore. Somewhere off the Danish coast it came on to blow as forecast. Our reefing gear broke so that we had to sail on under full mainsail.

In order to shift to a smaller jib, we ran before the wind straight inshore. There was a bright lighthouse straight ahead; this was somewhat alarming, as I did not know exactly how much sea room we had. At last, as the coast started to trend a bit more easterly, we could ease our sheets. We then sailed fast for the Skaw. Once we overtook a large steamer on the same course. After rounding the Skaw, we had a good run to Copenhagen, where we saw our German rival. She was considerably damaged, having lost the whole of her bulwarks on one side, her topmast and her spinnaker boom. But she had won the race and we were second. Most of our competitors had given up and gone through the Kiel Canal.

At Copenhagen Mollie and her sister joined us, and also Captain Ejnar Mikkelsen, the last of the ancient régime of Polar explorers. His first expedition was in the nineties. We sailed on to the Island of Bornholm in the Baltic. Here Mikki, as we call the captain, brought us in to his little home port of Gudjheim. We met there Mikki's step-son Sven, who later married my sister-in-law Pam.

We sailed back by way of the Danish Island of Anholt (where the drunks used to be put), the Swedish town of Maarstrand (where we got shut in the castle) and Oslo, finally heading for home from Christiansand in South Norway. Most of the way we had a strong Northerly wind. We drove her hard and made Burnham in three and a half days. One twenty-four hour run was over one hundred and sixty miles.

About this time *Duet* won the Town Cup at Burnham.

One cold winter day we were sailing in the Blackwater. It was foggy. Suddenly Jack Bedford said he thought he could hear a hail in the distance. We chugged over with our auxiliary engine to where he pointed, and found a boat capsized and two men in the water. It was a job for the two of us to get them aboard, as one was unconscious. The other was a large man, a doctor whom I recognized. We got him below into my bunk, where I rubbed him down with olive oil. I hoped to be able to revive him sufficiently to tell me what to do about the other fellow; Jack Bedford had meanwhile set to work on deck giving him artificial respiration. I could not get a word out of my man; he was blue with cold. I then set course full speed for West Mersea. There I put her on the mud as the quickest means of bringing up, and rowed ashore to get a doctor. He turned up quickly. I rowed him off and he immediately put an injection into the old man. But it was no good: he was dead. He turned out to be Sooty Mussett, the well-known wildfowler.

In 1935, as I was going to Greenland, I chartered the boat to my old friend, James Bacon.

Once we thought we would do a spring cruise to see Snowdon from the sea. We sailed away from Burnham in early April. The warm weather of March had changed and there was ice on the deck. As we approached Dover, a horrible-looking green squall appeared over the cliffs. We shortened down and it rained and hailed and blew. We put into the harbour where we were weatherbound for days. With me were my old friend Peter Rodd and his friend Evelyn Waugh. Their company was the only redeeming feature of the situation. At last, the weather seeming a little better, we sailed; it soon came on to blow again, however, and we put in to Boulogne. There we made fast to the floating Yacht Club and a tug. During the night it blew furiously and the Yacht Club disappeared. Luckily, the tug held. In the morning some Frenchmen came along and wanted to know what we had done with their Yacht Club. Peter dealt with them. They vanished. We were held up there for several days by the weather. At last we sailed again and managed to make Teignmouth. After bumping on the bar, we got into the harbour and secured to the buoys. Here Evelyn sent himself a telegram saying that he was required elsewhere on urgent business. I don't blame him. We sailed again, but off the Start it came on to blow very suddenly. The wind was right ahead and we had to take five rolls in the mainsail. We put into Plymouth where Mollie joined me. That was as far as we got, for time had run out and we had to return. It was an unsuccessful trip.

One day when we were out watching the big class racing in the Solent, we saw the extraordinary sight of the whole class running in line abreast up the Solent, all with spinnakers set. There was the famous old *Britannia*, the *Shamrock* and three or four others. Besides these cutters, there was the great schooner *Westward*—250 tons. In order to keep out of the way we steered inside the guardship—a large battleship anchored off Cowes. As we were doing this, we saw, to our concern, the *Westward* alter course and swiftly follow us. We pulled in our sheets and sailed as close to the battleship as we could without actually fouling the boat booms, which she had rigged out. The *Westward* came tearing astern of us, her immense mainboom squared right off; it seemed inevitable that her boom would strike our starboard shrouds, in which case we would certainly have been dismasted. The faces of rows of men lying on her decks peered at us over the bulwarks. Not a word was spoken. At last, when there seemed a mere matter of inches to go, a voice (I suppose it was the Skipper's) sang out from for'ard, "Luff sir, for God's sake, luff." Her steersman moved the wheel one spoke: the *Westward*'s boom drew out a foot and she rushed by.

Duet *at Cowes in 1936.*

We did two cruises in Brittany and visited some lovely anchorages. Two of the best on the North coast are up the rivers Lézardrieux and Tréguier. It was at one or other of these that a carrier pigeon came on board. This in itself is not an unusual thing to happen, but our bird stayed with us a fortnight. Every time we went ashore, it put its head over the rail and waited for us to come back. When we were down below we would hear it walking about on deck. We began to think it was going to stay with us and that we would take it home. But one day, the wind having changed, it took off, and, after flying round in circles a few times, set off for England.

On another trip we sailed to the west coast of Brittany, where we found some good langoustine. We had an uneasy time getting round Penmarch Point. Jack Bedford said, "Well, I suppose we must be under the lee of America," and quoted the oft-told saying: "Them as go to sea for pleasure would go to hell for pastime."

In 1939 we sailed to Norway, making a direct passage from Burnham to Bergen. We then went through the fjords and leads as far as Trondheim. From there we sailed to Shetland, making the port of Lerwick in a thick fog, and thence home down the east coast.

Duet did not have much to do during the War. She had a time of service as an obstruction moored in the river Crouch to stop sea planes landing. Her store ashore was invaded by mice, which after finishing a deposit of sugar next door began on our jerseys and cushions.

After the war ended we fitted her out again. Jack Bedford, who had served with the Merchant Service all the war, had gone elsewhere. Two of my best sailing companions were killed in the war. One was James Martin. He was a first-rate seaman as well as being a very strong fellow. He had been Bos'n in the *Discovery* on her voyage to the Antarctic and had served in many ships; he was Ryder's mate in the *Penola* with John Rymill's expedition to the Antarctic in 1934-37. On our last trip to Norway before the war, he was one of the crew. In the first part of the war, Martin was Ryder's First Lieutenant on a large "Q" ship which was torpedoed in the Atlantic. Ryder himself survived, having on a blow-up waistcoat which kept him afloat for four days. The other companion whom I missed very much was Michael Spender. He was a most intelligent and useful man, who spent most of his time climbing and mapping in the Himalayas. He could always tell you what the weather was going to do by reference to the higher air. He knew about literature and music and was an ideal companion. After being in Intelligence for most of the war, he was killed flying in France on almost the last day. The pilot survived.

When *Duet* was fitted out again we took on an old boy called Ernie Cardnell. For many years he had been skipper of a Thames barge, but he was caught by a blitz in the London Docks, and, thinking that this was too much of a good thing, retired. All the same, Cardnell could not stay long away from the water and so he came to us as ship keeper. He never could get used to the way of a yacht, and always thought it was highly dangerous being at sea. Once, when it got a bit jumpy outside, he said to Mollie, "Us never ought to have went out of the river, Mother." One night, when we were on passage to France it came on to blow in the Thames Estuary. We were reefing down and old Cardnell was supposed to be turned in in the fo'csle. Suddenly I heard a noise behind me and, turning round, saw a pair of hands clinging to the rail. He had gone over the side while trying to give us a hand. When we got to France, the "peaked caps" wanted to know all our ages. I asked Cardnell for his. He didn't know but thought he might be eighty-two.

We did a trip to the Deben river. On the way we passed the Rough Tower—one of the anti-aircraft towers put in the Thames Estuary during the War. Cardnell, whose eyes were failing, spent a long time gazing at it. At last he turned to me and said: "I reckon that's one of them French smacks, ain't it, sir?" Coming out of the Deben it was a bit bumpy. We suddenly found that we were filling with water and hastily put back. It was a leak in the stern gland.

Another trip we did was to the river Alde. It is considered inadvisable to enter without a pilot, as there is a difficult bar which is always shifting. We hove to off the entrance with our Pilot flag hoisted. After waiting about two hours, nobody appeared. By this time it was nearly high water; I decided to enter on my own. With two of my boys as leadsmen—one on each side—we sailed in and up the river past the Island of Avocets and the old Norman castle of Orford; we dropped our anchor at Aldeburgh. Another day we sailed up the river to Iken. All was well, except that the heads went wrong.

The time came when we had to leave Cardnell ashore; he was getting too old and he could not see.

In 1947 we took a house for the summer holidays near Loch Moidart. We sailed there through the Pentland Firth round the north of Scotland. Mollie and Christopher joined me for the return passage. It was after we had rounded Cape Wrath that Chris got a bad sore throat. We put into Thurso where a doctor, who came aboard, said we could continue the passage but it would be better if Chris went overland. We passed through the Pentland, doing about thirteen knots over the ground, and altered course for the south at Duncansby Head. As the wind came ahead we went ashore at Stonehaven; Chris found that he was very weak walking. We sailed again first thing in the morning on our way home. A large basking shark appeared and we nearly ran into it. It came on to blow pretty hard but the wind was fair. One night the man at the helm let her come up into the wind. She heeled right over creating a certain amount of havoc in the galley and shipping a sea through the after skylight into Mollie's bunk.

When we were off the coast of Northumberland, Chris developed a shocking headache which would not respond to aspirin. Clearly there was something seriously wrong and we pushed on for the nearest port, Blyth. There was a light head wind which made slow going. When we put on the engine it made his headache worse; when we shut it off, we stood still. At last we got to Blyth and entered harbour flying the flag for a doctor. The port doctor came aboard and pronounced that Chris had a disease of the gums and that we had better get a dentist. The one we got turned out to be a man I had met before; he had taken out our Doc's tooth when we were in the

Quest in 1930. He said there was nothing wrong with Chris's teeth or his gums but that he was seriously ill and recommended a good doctor in Newcastle.

Dr. Boon came out. He said that Chris had either got Polio or TB Meningitis. If it was the latter it would be fatal. He could not tell which it was until he had made tests and said he could do nothing for him aboard the boat. We had some difficulty in getting Chris ashore and into an ambulance to be taken to a nursing home in Newcastle. But we managed it in the end and we waited at the nursing home for the verdict. After a couple of days we got it: Polio. It was some weeks before he was sufficiently recovered to be moved by train to London.

In the meantime, my crew had evaporated. I managed to get hold of my old friend Frank Carr to help me get *Duet* home. We sailed one night in November. After rounding Flamborough Head the weather came on bad. There was a very nasty looking sky to windward and it started to blow. We pushed inshore and anchored off the Lincolnshire coast, giving her thirty fathoms of cable. It blew very hard all night. We rolled heavily but did not drag.

By morning we had good weather and a fair wind. We made a quick passage to the Norfolk coast, then ran into big thunder storms and heavy rain. Passing Yarmouth about midnight, we made a signal home through Lloyds' signal station. Picking up the first of the flood at Yarmouth, in a few hours we were sailing up the Crouch to our moorings at Burnham.

Two years later we set out for Jamaica, where Chris would be able to get some warm-water swimming after the operation he had had to his back following his attack of Polio. It was the most perfect summer imaginable. We had a fine weather cruise down the French coast to the Channel Islands and then across to Teignmouth. We did not leave there until October, and after a long, tiresome passage across the Bay with headwinds all the way, arrived at Corunna in

Spain. There we had to have repaired a certain amount of damage to the gear aloft and the split sails. We mobilized a "chippy" and sailmaker to do the work but found we had not enough money, so we went to the British Vice-Consul to see what could be done about it. He said he was very sorry but he had strict orders from the British Government that yachts were not to have any money. The firm which had tried unsuccessfully to repair our wireless wanted ten pounds. This we had not got; we told them, through the Vice-Consul, that they could have five pounds up to midnight but after that nothing. The firm retaliated by getting the Captain of the port to arrest the ship and inform us in writing that we must not leave the port until all accounts had been paid.

We went off to dine at the Club, leaving the boat covered up. There was a guard on the quay. At midnight we came back quietly, took off the covers and sailed. The guard, by this time, was fast asleep on the quay.

By next morning we were butting into a strong south wester. This increased to gale force with low ugly clouds. Cape Finisterre seemed as far away as ever. For several days we either lay hove to, or tried to get to windward under the trysail. Then I realized that it was no good going on. I had promised my crew that they would get back for Christmas. If I went on, I should be left singlehanded after we reached Jamaica. So the only thing to do was to put the helm up and run for home.

It was blowing a full gale but it was a fair wind. We ran under trysail and our little pocket handkerchief spitfire jib. After a few hours, it was clear we were running too fast. We handed our trysail and paid out warps astern. When I came on deck at four a.m. to take over the morning watch, I did not like the look of it. The glass was falling fast and there was a very heavy sea. We handed the "spitfire" and, running under bare poles, kept her dead before the sea. Even with nothing set, she was doing six knots. I was just thinking how well she was steering when all of a sudden we seemed to be overwhelmed. We had been pooped. I was swept away from the helm and out of the cockpit; luckily we have life rails which stopped me from going overboard. The whole deck had disappeared under water. She broached to, and I let her lie with the helm lashed down. The mizzen boom had been smashed, but no other damage was visible. Soon, however, one of the crew came up from below to tell me that the batteries had been carried away and so had the cabin table. We lay well enough broadside to the sea with no way on. *Duet* was heeled over by the force of the wind on her masts. The trouble was that she would not come up enough to get the sea on her bow. Water kept on breaking over the side and getting down the after skylight; we manned the pump and had to keep it going all the time. The force of the wind was such that, shouting at the top of your voice from the companion-way, you could not make the helmsman hear you; this at a distance of about ten feet. We put out oil bags, got our heavy towing warp up from the sail locker, secured it to the mast and paid it out over the bow. We also lashed a small hatch cover in the mizzen rigging. This brought her head up a point or so and she rode perfectly, taking no more water aboard.

There was nothing more we could do on deck, so we all went below. One of us would stick his head up every quarter of an hour to see if a steamer was coming, but the spindrift made it impossible to see far. The glass was still falling. Then, after reaching the lowest I had ever seen, it started to rise. The wind went to the west and blew harder than ever. After a bit we found that we could no longer get up the companion-way. The mainsail, which was stowed on the boom, had got full of water and was weighing down in a heavy bag. We had to cut it hole in it to let out the water.

The storm died down the next day and we could once more set our course for England. Some days later we sighted the Start from the masthead. I remember it was a Sunday and we held a little thanksgiving service on deck.

We put in to Brixham, with our cabin table on deck, to get some of our damage repaired. This done, we sailed up Channel for Burnham. After putting in to Ramsgate, we sailed one November morning at four a.m. We got ashore on the Dike shoal. It was blowing on shore. The lifeboat came out to us, but we managed to get off without her help. The people at Burnham were very surprised to see us back.

A year or two later, my boy Christopher, decided to go in for the Public School Dragon class racing on the Clyde. He asked me to take *Duet* up there to provide a base ship. In order to arrive in time for the races, we went through that smelly sewer, the Forth and Clyde Canal. There were thirty-nine locks, which we had to help to work ourselves. Once they let out too much water and we stuck right in the middle; another time, when we got to the far end, we found a railway bridge which would not open. We had to wait until it was repaired. After the Dragon racing, we came home by the Caledonian and sailed back by the east coast.

We had made various improvements since the war. These included:

1. A new silver spruce hollow mast. This replaced the original solid pitch pine one, which is now stepped on the lawn at Spencers. The new mast saved a lot of weight aloft, and with it *Duet* was much less tender.
2. New decks. The original kauri pine decks had become leaky and thin. Teak was unobtainable, so we had the new decks made of a similar wood from Africa called "Aphramosia".
3. A diesel engine. The old petrol engine was always being put out of action by sea water. I got very tired of it having to be taken to pieces and spread out on my bunk. We installed a V-Twin Turner Diesel of fifteen horse-power with a self-starter. This has proved excellent.

In 1955, being somewhat incapacitated by neuritis, I signed on a skipper, Navvy Mussett of Tollesbury. He comes of a famous line of fishermen; there are Mussett tombs in the churchyard that go back to the fifteen hundreds. For a good many generations, they have been called "Navvy", father and son. (This, I think, was the nickname given to one who was navigator of a sailing ship.)

I had never sailed in warm water and thought it was about time I did, so I decided to take *Duet* to the Mediterranean.

We sailed from West Mersea early in July and had a good fair wind as far as the Isle of Wight, whither we ran under our squaresail. Then we had flat calms all the way to Cornwall and had to use the engine. After storing and watering we left Fowey towards the end of July. We soon picked up a fine, fresh north-easter. In four days we were in Vigo—all the way under the squaresail, never setting the mainsail once.

Then on to Gibraltar by the lovely coast of Portugal and the Berling Islands. The advice of Signor Pereira, the Portuguese Ambassador in London, was a great help to us on this coast. At Lisbon we were joined by Chris, who had been sailing with Lord Merthyr in his barge on the coast of France and the north coast of Spain. We went ashore here to see the lovely old convent of St. Geronimo near our berth, at Belem. It is the burial-place of Vasco da Gama.

At Gibraltar we were received with great ceremony by the Queen's Harbour Master and the Officer of the Guard, as we were flying the white ensign. There my passage crew left me and our sons Julien and William joined (Stephen had just had his appendix out and was to join later at Palma). Chris now took on the navigation. We sailed to Malaga in company with another yacht, *Lady Elspeth,* that we had met at Gibraltar. She sailed some hours before we did, but we caught her up and entered harbour in line abreast. There I went ashore in my wheel chair to see the wonderful Cathedral; the boys went to a bullfight. We then sailed along the south coast of Spain, making for the Balearic Islands. We put in at Port Morril where the crew hired a car to take them to Granada. Here they had a good look at the famous Alhambra.

We had no sooner dropped our anchor in San Pedro Bay than our companion, the *Lady Elspeth*, arrived; we had not seen her for some days. San Pedro is a deserted little bay inhabited only by a few police—there is no road, telegraph or telephone. We were held up here for about five days while the Levanter blew. The *Lady Elspeth* got bored and ran back to Gibraltar. After putting in at Cartagena, where the local opinion was that the weather would go on being bad, we sailed for Majorca. Not far from the island, we met a very fierce-looking waterspout and quickly got down the little canvas we had set. The waterspout faded away.

At length we came to the Balearics and sailed through the narrow channel between Ibiza and Formentera, reaching the harbour at Palma at six in the morning. The Cathedral looked magnificent in the early light. The boys had to tow in with a dinghy, our engine being out of action.

Here my boy Stephen joined, and also Mrs. Brady, the wife of one of the crew.

After taking stores we went on to the small island of Cabrera. Here there was a sheltered bay, unlighted, which we entered at night; we could, however, make out the old castle on the hill in the moonlight. Chris was the navigator.

From this island we set our course for Minorca. But, the wind heading us, we made for the bay Formentor. There we anchored in about three fathoms, in what looked like sand but was actually pumice. About three in the morning the mistral came on and we soon found that we had dragged right across the bay. We got the engine going and went back to our original anchorage under the lee of the shore. Although we put out two anchors with plenty of cable, we found we dragged just as before; there was by now a lot of wind.

Eventually we had to run *Duet* ashore on the weather side in order to stay put.

We had intended to go on round the island by the north coast. But, the mistral blowing right on shore, we decided to go back to Palma by the way we had come. The first night we put in to Port Ratjada. Sailing from there early next morning, we got back to Palma that evening.

All the time in the Mediterranean it was very hot. In harbour we used to rig our awnings, but at sea the deck was unprotected from the sun. At Palma the boys went to another bullfight. They were lucky in sitting just behind Ivan Ivanovic, who could speak English; he was a great expert on bullfights and could explain all the intricacies to them.

After a day or two we took *Duet* to Port Andraix, where we left her in Mussett's charge, taking on a Spanish caretaker called Lorenzo to look after her during the winter. Then we flew home, arriving back in early September.

Duet.

August Courtauld up Duet's *mainmast.*

15

The Navy

RNVSR, The Admiralty and Coastal Forces

WHEN I got home from Greenland in 1935, I found the Abyssinian War starting up. It seemed to me that men who knew a bit about the sea ought to be allowed to give a hand in the Navy. I got out a scheme whereby we might help, using our own ships, and went to see the Admiral Commanding Reserves. He did not sound at all hopeful, but said he would consult "the powers that be" in the Admiralty. Some time later he asked me to come and see him. He explained that he had consulted all the Staff Departments; they had said that there would be no small craft in the next war. The only way in which the Admiral thought we could help was by sitting in the bowels of a trawler listening in to head-phones. He told me that this was the great secret of the Navy, called "Asdic". It seemed the Navy wanted, for this purpose, men who would not be seasick all the time.

Nothing much came of this for quite a long time, but eventually the First Lord (Samuel Hoare) announced that a new reserve would be created: "The Royal Naval Volunteer Supplementary Reserve." There would be no uniform, no training and no pay. It would simply be a list.

When the time came I went along to HMS *President* on the Embankment to enrol. After a short interview and a medical inspection, I was signed on.

I went to the Admiral Commanding Reserves to ask if we could have some training in the ways of the Navy, even if this were only instruction by a Petty Officer on a Saturday afternoon. The answer was "*No*". It seemed that the Navy hadn't got any money, and that, even if they had, they would spend it on something else.

Later they invented groups for the RNVSR; I was asked to take over one which was called "The East Anglian Group", but I was given no authority. They also got the Board of Trade to examine for a new type of Yacht Master's Certificate.

I got together with my old friend Frank Carr and we enlisted a gang of fellows who had joined the RNVSR and who lived in East Anglia. To help them pass this new "ticket" he gave them lectures once a week in London, while I did the same in Essex. We tried to teach them signalling, navigation and seamanship.

At last the Board of Trade were ready to examine. The examination took three days. There were written papers in Magnetism, Chart work and Meteorology; there was an eye test and an examination in signalling—morse, semaphore and International Code. You had to know all the flags and the single flag meanings by heart. But the most fearsome part was the oral exam, in which you went alone before a Board of Trade examiner who put models and coloured lights on the table. He kept up a running fire of questions, asking what you would do in every conceivable circumstance. You were expected to know by heart all the articles for the "prevention of collisions at sea". I managed to draw the examiner off by yarning about fogs. By the time we had finished swapping our fogs, the interview was over. I found to my surprise that I had passed.

We conducted exercises in our own boats as station-keeping under sail was tricky, with vessels of different types and sizes, and we had no one to help us. I remember that we passed a signal about Mussolini's invasion of Albania round our little flotilla.

War came. We all listened keenly to the wireless to hear when we were going to be called up. It seemed that everybody but us was being ordered to their posts. The RNVSR was not mentioned. After a bit the fellows in my group started telephoning to ask what was happening. I could tell them nothing. A week or two went by; then I could stand it no longer. I sent a telegram to the Admiral Commanding Reserves suggesting that a stand-by message should be sent out, as members of my group were considering joining other services. There was no reply until next day, when a letter came reading: "The Admiral Commanding Reserves desires me to state that if you wish to resign from the RNVSR, he will accept your resignation forthwith." My answer was to the effect that I had no intention of resigning, and requested to be called up. It never occurred to us that the Navy did not want us, but that was the case.

For the last year or two I had been doing for an organization which I called "the crooked people" some work which included a survey of all the northern coasts of Europe. Frank Carr and I had got together a gang of fellows who went off in their boats in the summer of '39. We covered the coasts of the southern half of Norway, West Sweden, Denmark, Holland and Belgium, and sent in our reports. Whether any use was made of them I never heard.

These people now gave me instructions to proceed to a town in the Midlands and there see a certain Naval Commander. I reached this place by car and asked a policeman the way to the address I had been given. He looked so highly suspicious I was afraid he was going to put me inside. At length, however, I found my objective, a large country house standing in a park near the town. I discovered my Commander in a secluded part of the grounds. He proceeded to explain how a new type of magnetic bomb worked, and gave it to me to take away in a suitcase.

In London, I was told to take the thing to Swansea, where I was to hand it over to the captain of a certain ship and explain how it worked. He was going to Gibraltar where he would swim with the bomb to a ship in which it appeared we were taking an interest. The bomb would stick to the ship by magnets. After a timed delay, the thing would go off and make a hole in the side of the ship.

I proceeded to the Naval Base at Swansea, where I found myself treated politely but with suspicion. I could not tell them what it was all about. Having penetrated the Docks, I made my way to the ship carrying my bomb. Getting the captain in his cabin, I explained the working of the infernal machine, how it was fused and how the time delay worked.

I was told to remain at Swansea, and for a few days hung about the Naval Base. At that time (October 1939) the first ship to be hit by a magnetic mine was brought into dry dock. In company with other officers from the base, I walked underneath her. Her bottom was wrinkled in waves and it was clear that she had not actually been in contact with any normal mine. It seemed to me that the only answer was a magnetic mine. At that time these machines had not been heard of. A few days later I was told to go back to the captain of the ship and tell him to throw the machine overboard. I was then to return to London.

August Courtauld as a member of Section D, "the crooked people", the precursor of SOE (Special Operations Executive).

⁎   ⁎   ⁎

After this I was fixed up with a desk in the Naval Intelligence Division in the Admiralty. I was to act as liaison officer with my "crooked" friends, and I found myself on Admiral Godfrey's staff in the famous room 39.

After a time, I was transferred to the Balkan Section. This consisted of a retired Commander and a young Captain of Marines. We were supposed to be laying plans for dropping mines in the Danube. Later I was shifted to the German Section. This included Scandinavia, as well as most of Europe.

The ignorance of the NID was fantastic. There was a very nice man I worked with on Scandinavia, called Mr. Todd. He was a great expert on Egypt, having been Cooks' Agent in Cairo for many years. He had never been to Scandinavia; however, he was a very calm and competent fellow, and he did it very well.

One day, my chief, the Naval Commander of the section, told me to find out the latest news of the Swedish Fleet. I hunted through the files and brought in the result. It was dated several years previously and said that "owing to an outbreak of foot and mouth disease the manœuvres of the Swedish main fleet would be cancelled". He roared with laughter.

At this time the Admiralty was much exercised to know how the Germans were getting home all their big merchant ships. Their Lordships could not believe that it was possible for a ship to go through the Denmark Strait between Iceland and Greenland in the winter, or that a big ship could navigate the Inner Lead down the coast of Norway.

One day, I was told that DDOH wanted to see me immediately. I did not know who this person was or where to find him, but I set out into the labyrinth thinking I should see these mysterious letters on a door. After many enquiries, I did in fact arrive. Behind the door was an office housing a naval captain. His name was Harcourt, his title Deputy Director Operations (Home). (He has since become an Admiral and Commander in Chief at The Nore.) Straightway he said, pointing to a large chart on the wall: "Can a ship get between Iceland and Greenland in the winter?" I replied: "Yes, sir, it could." He said: "Well! how the devil do you think I am going to find the cruisers to do all that?"

I discovered later a book of charts, utterly secret, of course, which gave the position of the ice for every month of the year. This showed a white blank between Iceland and Greenland during the winter months, which meant that the strait was impassable.

Frank Carr was sent up to Grimsby to get information about the ice from the trawler skippers. He got together a number who, after some time, agreed on a statement. This declared that there was a channel with an average width of forty miles between Iceland and the Greenland pack in the winter. In fact, it is only in most exceptional years that the pack reaches the coast of Iceland.

At this time, Winston Churchill, who was First Lord, kept on sending out submarines and other naval forces to catch the German ships coming down the coast of Norway. He was specially interested in the iron ore ships coming from Narvik; no one ever saw one of these ships. It was not until we got the report of a British captain who had come down the Inner Lead in a big ship—under the charge, as usual, of Norwegian pilots—and who had taken sufficient interest in the navigation to plot his track, that we could establish with certainty that the Inner Lead was navigable by large ships.

We used to take turns on duty at night. This mostly amounted to locking up the innumerable safes, burning the paper and ordering supper. It used to take a quarter of an hour to lock the safes. So far as I know, no one ever looked in them. Most of the contents were marked, anyhow, with such instructions as *"Not to be read by anyone"*.

On one occasion when I was on duty at night with a Major of Marines who was second in command in our section, there was a noise of someone running down the stairs (we were in the basement). A frenzied man burst in. "Do you do Spitzbergen here?" he asked. "Afraid not, old boy," the major replied. "Try upstairs in the American section."

About this time the Norwegian Campaign started. A special room was created for Norway, and I was put in charge. Luckily I had a set of my own Norwegian charts and a good German atlas. There seemed to be no atlases in the Admiralty.

At the beginning of the War, Frank Carr and I went to the Hydrographer to beg him to put back on the Admiralty charts the dotted line showing the marked shipping track. We had both sailed in Norway and knew that, without this, it was impossible to find one's way through the maze of rocks which line the coast. The reply was that the decision had been taken some time before to remove the dotted line, and that this could not be changed. Soon after the Norwegian campaign started, a British cruiser was lost on a rock on the coast of Norway; there was a scream from the Fleet for Norwegian charts. The Navy only possessed one copy of these charts, and this was at Bath. It took some time to print others and send them to the Fleet.

One day, I was told by my senior officer to take an Admiralty car, pick up a chief constable from Scotland Yard and take him to the docks where he wanted to interview somebody; a Dutchman, I think. I did this and brought him back. A few days later a senior civil servant in the department called me into his room. "What do you mean by taking Admiralty cars?" he said. "Buses and tubes are good enough for you."

When I first went to the Admiralty I was wearing plain clothes; everyone was very polite. But soon I was commissioned as a temporary probationary Sub-Lieutenant, RNVR. My pay was nine shillings per day. The smiles faded from their faces when they saw my sleeve.

This chair-borne work might be all very interesting, but it was not what I joined the Navy for. I must get out somehow, I thought. Requests to higher authority seemed to have no effect, so I came to the conclusion that the only thing to do was to fail to answer questions. One day a sharp voice asked me something on the telephone. I recognized the voice of Shorty, the ADNI. "I'm afraid I don't know," I replied. "Is there a bloody fool on the end of this line?" came back. "Yes, sir!" I said.

*   *   *

At last I escaped from the sacred portals. It was the time of Dunkirk. I was on leave and asked if I could go and pour out tea for the troops at Dover; they said that they had plenty of hands.

By now I was a Lieutenant and I was sent to the Royal Naval College at Greenwich to learn how to be an executive officer. It was all very pleasant; we dined in the Painted Hall. When I left they asked me what I would like to do; I said, "Navigation in a cruiser."

One day, my old friend Admiral Goodenough came to have lunch with me. He had come down to address the WRNS. I asked him if he was going to tell them about the Battle of Jutland. "No, my boy, nothing of the kind," said he. "I shall tell them about Life, just Life." The last time I saw him was after having lunch with him in the Haymarket. I walked to Piccadilly tube station to see him off, asked him where he was going and, having found out his route, said "Good-bye", from the top of the escalator. "You follow the red light, Admiral," I told him as he disappeared. "I always do," he replied. I never saw him again.

The appointments people at the Admiralty told me to go to MTBs; they said that in three weeks I would get a command. I joined HMS *Hornet* at Gosport to take the MTB course. Soon I found myself First Lieutenant of an MTB; we used to pirouette in this, in the Solent. One

108

day when we were out, the first air raid on Portsmouth happened; the whole town seemed to be covered in dense smoke, and there were explosions. We opened fire on the enemy planes with our 0.5 machine guns, without much effect. The best shooting was done by two Polish destroyers. They brought down at least one plane.

At *Hornet* there seemed to be a lot of young RN Officers whose ships had been lost at Dunkirk, waiting for commands. Very few boats were being built, and the Admiralty's idea that an RNVR officer could get a command in three weeks was evidently optimistic. I remember remarking at breakfast that the trouble with the Navy was that officers no longer sank with their ships. This didn't contribute to my popularity. Eventually I was given the command of MAC2, one of the original MTB flotilla which had gone out to Malta before the war, and had come home through the French canals. The ship had had her torpedo tubes removed and one of her engines, but she still had two Napier Lions, each of 500 hp, and could do thirty knots. She also had the distinction of having in her crew the oldest sailor in the Navy—Jock Lamont.

August Courtauld (far right) and the crew of MAC2.

We were sent to Dover to escort mine-sweepers, but soon became a rescue boat instead, picking up airmen when they crashed in their planes. Our base was the Lord Warden Hotel, known as HMS *Wasp*.

I sometimes used to go up to the Castle to see my master, the Captain of Minesweepers. There I discovered that the Admiral was looking at the Germans on the French coast with an ordinary signalman's telescope. I offered his Chief of Staff the loan of a large astronomical telescope that I happened to have at home, if he could let me have the petrol to go and fetch it when I next had a day off. He said that they would like to have it and he would go and see the paymaster about the petrol. He returned to say that no petrol could be granted. Later, I had the instrument sent by rail. The Admiral, Bertram Ramsay, had it put up on his balcony in the cliffs under the castle, where it remained for the rest of the War.

My crew always said that if we ever picked up a German airman there was nothing they wouldn't do to him. One day we did pick up a German near Dungeness. He was an officer who had commanded a bomber which was brought down on its way back from a raid on London, and he was wearing the Iron Cross. I gave my revolver to Jock Lamont, telling him to take the man for'ard and bring me anything he had got. When we got back to Dover I handed over to my coxswain and went down to the forecastle to have a look at the prisoner. I asked Jock how he was doing. The answer was, "Ssh, sir! We've given him a nice cup of tea and he's just gone off to sleep." When we had landed our officer, he was marched off by an armed guard of soldiers with fixed bayonets. My crew thought it was very cruel.

One day, after the Admiral had a notice put up closing the port and saying that no vessels were to leave harbour, my boat was seen going out at full speed. When I was asked by the Commanding Officer of the Base why I had done this, I replied, "Well, sir, I have a strict rule in my life, that I never read notices." The officer commanding a ship expects to get his orders by signal from his Admiral.

MAC2 moved to Ramsgate. We continued doing Air-Sea Rescue in conjunction with the RAF. Most of our searches were near the Goodwins, which were littered with wrecks. The only time we found a British airman, he was dead. Unlike the German Air Force, the RAF did not supply self-inflating lifebelts, and air crews had neither the time nor the energy to blow up their lifebelts by mouth. To make matters worse, the information we got of the position of a falling airman was very vague. By the time the usual delays had occurred, the man would be many miles away, for the tides run strongly in those parts. We used to lie stationary, rolling off the North Foreland, whenever air operations were on. Then we would get a signal and quickly steam to the position given. One day, when we were lying in our waiting position, the coast guns opened fire. Shells started to come rather too close. We asked permission to move. It turned out that Winston had come down to inspect the coast defences; he couldn't resist letting off the guns.

The first time we took up our new station at Ramsgate I sent this telegram to Mollie: "Come where the boy sheep passes."

One day when we were returning through the Thames Estuary from Felixstowe, where we had to go for our refits, a large explosion went off in the sea astern of us. There were some naval vessels nearby, and I thought they must have produced it. When we got back to Dover, the Admiralty rang up: they wanted to know about the acoustic mine I had let off. I was thankful that I had been going pretty fast and therefore it had gone off well astern.

After a year or so I was given the command of a new motor gunboat. I took her over at the builder's yard (Scott-Paine's) at Hythe, near Southampton.

Coastal forces had depended on the Italian Isotta-Fraschini engine. It was a beautiful bit of machinery which developed about 1200 hp. In spite of all requests, the Admiralty refused to buy the licence to make these engines in England. Italy entered the war against us; there were no more engines, and therefore no more MTBs or MGBs. However, that genius Scott-Paine went over to Canada to get a brand new engine design. In less than a year the new Packard engines were coming over. They were of 1350 hp.

I had three Packards in my new boat; she did forty-five knots.

After acceptance trials I took her to Portland to be based on HMS *Attack*. On the way it was blowing hard and I was driving her into a heavy sea. My coxswain, who was at the wheel, hit his head on the roof of the armoured wheelhouse and was knocked out.

A bit later I was playing about somewhere near St. Alban's Head, doing something like thirty-five knots, when suddenly the boat felt as if she were breaking in half. We immediately stopped all three engines and discovered that one of the blades had come off the centre propeller. After we got her on the slip, we found that all the propellers were eaten through by electrolytic action due to the fact that bronze propellers had been fitted on steel shafts. It looked as if the propeller blades had been eaten at the roots by worms. The admiralty designers had forgotten the old sailors' dodge of dealing with this trouble by nailing a piece of zinc on to the hull.

It was a long time before I got my new propellers. When they came, I sailed in company with some other MGBs for my operational base at Lowestoft. By this time the Thames Estuary was so thick with wrecks, sunk by magnetic and acoustic mines, that the pilots found great difficulty in getting any more ships into the river.

While I was at Dover I put up a plan for dealing with this to the torpedo officer on the Admiral's staff. My idea was that the Admiralty should take over a lot of Thames sailing barges, which could tow a noise-making machine on a long hawser, tacking backwards and forwards across the channels in the Thames Estuary. As the barges would make no mechanical noise themselves, they would be safe, but the noise devices would explode the mines. The officer replied that the Admiralty knew all about it, that it was no business of mine, and that he could not forward the idea.

However, the wrecks did not worry us, and we duly arrived at Lowestoft, but only to find the harbour closed because a ship had sunk in the entrance. We went further north.

This brought us to the headquarters of a Flag Officer who was a bit of a character. His ship was a "stone frigate" (a naval base ashore)—and the original naval lunatic asylum. He used to have weekly Commanding Officers' Conferences (woe betide anyone who was late!), and at these he presided, looking just like a Bateman Admiral. At one of these confabs he announced that our reports of the enemies' position muddled up his plot—a situation chart kept up to date by WRNS. He said that all we were doing was to sight one another, and that we were not to make enemy reports east of a certain longitude. We had always been told that the last thing to do before sinking was to make an enemy report. His veto, therefore, contravened King's Regulations.

Weymouth Bay, November 1941.

Soon we moved to Lowestoft by the Broads, where we were based on HMS *Mantis*, Our operations were always at night and usually consisted of taking up a patrol line laid down on the chart east of the convoy route. The E-boats used to come over to torpedo ships on the nightly convoys.

There were some very good fellows among the officers of the MGBs. One was the famous Hitch (Robert Hichens). He developed the tactics of stalking the E-boats at slow speed, and then engaging at very close range. Hitch was a tall fellow and was shot through the head standing on his bridge. Another of the officers, a special friend of mine, was Peter Bennett. He was sent off one night to a position not on his chart. He therefore went to the nearest one that was; this, unfortunately, was occupied by another boat from Yarmouth. They met, and he was killed by his own side, standing on his bridge. He also was a very tall man; he was a brilliant musician. Another casualty was Derek Leaf, also a fine young fellow much loved by his crew. "Those whom the gods love, die young."

The E-boats never used to come out in bad weather, nor when there was a moon. The Yarmouth staff, who controlled us, had not found this out. Whenever anything happened in the North Sea, even if it was only a mine going up, out we went. Very soon, with this continual operating in bad weather, my boat started to break up. The bowler hats from the Admiralty did not like the look of her, so I was ordered to take her to Brightlingsea and pay her off. Having done this, I was given another MGB with which I carried on at Lowestoft.

One night I thought I had found the enemy. There was a bright light just above the horizon to the east. I set off at full speed in chase. After a bit I realized it was Venus rising from the sea.

Later, one of the ML Commanding Officers falling ill, I was told to take over his ML. These were considerably bigger craft than the MGBs, but much slower; they had two engines of 850 hp. which gave them a top speed of eighteen knots.

In the MLs we used to escort the coastal convoys to and from the Humber. The difficulty was to go slow enough. The convoy frequently did under five knots; and even going dead slow on one engine we had to keep on stopping. When steaming against wind and tide, the unhandy merchant ships were sometimes unable to maintain steerage-way, and they used to get tied up with the swept-channel buoys.

The MLs were fitted with two torpedo tubes; with these we were intended to torpedo the German invasion. At length I was sent to Portland to try out my torpedoes. The passage round was easy enough, and when I arrived at the base I embarked a torpedo, all teed up and ready to fire with a practice head. These torpedos were chuckouts from the American Town-class destroyers. I went out into Weymouth Bay and let mine off. A few seconds later there was a yell from my look-out aft: the thing was coming straight for our stern. I went full ahead, hard aport, and it tore past heading for Portland Bill. Losing a torpedo is a serious matter. I knew this one would get into Portland Race and that it would be carried in long way by the tide. I worked out on the chart where I thought it would get to, rounded the Bill and picked it up.

When I got back to Lowestoft, an order came through from the Admiral that our gun shields were to be cut off. He announced at one of our weekly confabs that he knew we could never hit anything while cowering behind gun shields, and that he would do away with them. The guns were three pounders. Mine had a wonderful history sheet going back to 1882; it had served on the NW Frontier as part of a mule train, on a mine sweeper in the first war, and on a battleship as a saluting gun. Dockyard maties came and cut off the shields with blowpipes. Soon after, the bowler hats in the Armaments Department discovered this. They were furious and ordered them to be replaced instantly, so the shields were screwed on again with nuts and bolts.

Next, I was sent to Felixstowe to be based on HMS *Beehive*. I was Divisional Leader (second in command) of the sixth ML Flotilla. We carried on in the same routine, escorting the nightly convoys to the Humber and back. We used to leave the convoy off the Humber and make our own way up river to Immingham.

The Flotilla started a new base for itself at Pin Mill, up the Orwell, where we were very happy and independent. On Sundays we used to have Divisions ashore and march the men to church at Chelmondiston.

One day an Army officer came to see me. He said, "The soldiers want to have a battle; could we lay on a combined operation?" I replied, "Yes! of course," adding as an afterthought, "How many men do you want us to take?" "About a thousand," he said. I said nothing, but went straight off to HMS *Ganges* (the Naval training base at Shotley), where I saw the Captain and asked him for some whalers to move all these bodies. He sent for the Commander and asked him if he could provide this transport. The Commander did not like the idea at all; he said the soldiers would spoil his whalers with their dirty boots. Said the Captain, "Come, now, Commander, there's a war on." The whalers were provided, and we towed them up to Pin Mill.

On the night of the operation there was a thick September fog. The plan was to go up river to a jetty on the north-east side, embark the soldiers and take them across the river to their battle in Wolverstone Park. During the battle we were to provide a bombardment of blank cartridges with our three-pounders, and we were also to put ashore a naval landing party to take part in the battle.

It started badly. We all ran ashore on the mud going up the river in the fog. However, we got ourselves off, picked up the soldiers and took them across the river. We then started the bombardment. The trouble about this was that one of our boats had not managed to get any blanks. So they fired live rounds; and we heard afterwards that the soldiers, hearing the shells whistling through the trees, lay down to wait until it was over. Our Commando party, with blackened faces, were the first to get to the objective, where they met the umpire. He told them that if only he could have soldiers like them, he would be all right. They were tickled to death.

Mollie and the children were camping at Pin Mill at the time. Since our operation was, of course, wrapped in secrecy, the bombardment echoing amongst the woods caused a certain amount of stir in the village. They thought that the Germans had landed.

This secrecy business was all very well, but it had its drawbacks. An old friend of mine, who was in the NID, came down to Felixstowe while we were there. In conversation I asked him if he knew anything about the E-boats we were supposed to fight. We knew neither their speed nor armament; the only thing we did know was that we could never catch them. He replied, "Of course, we know it all!" Apparently the information had been sent down, but, being marked "secret", it was locked up in the safe at the Admiral's office. It was never passed to us and we were never any wiser.

Clandestine photograph of August Courtauld leaving
Felixstowe for Dover, taken by Mollie Courtauld.

16

The Navy

Arctic Commando, Atlantic Ferry, Destroyer and the Beer Ship

THE DAY came round when I got orders to go and see Red Ryder (Capt R. E. D. Ryder, VC) at the Admiralty. I had known him in the old days when he commanded the schooner *Penola* which took John Rymill's expedition to the Antarctic; taking her round from Southampton to London I had acted as one of his crew. "Red" told me that a new thing was to be started called "Arctic Commando". It was too secret for him to tell me what this was going to do, but it sounded very exciting.

I had to give up my command and went down to Pin Mill to hand over my ML. When I was rowed ashore for the last time, my crew cheered me. It brought a lump to my throat.

The first thing to learn was kayak rolling in a London swimming bath. Next I was told to go to a place on the west coast of Scotland to choose about twenty men. They were all new recruits to the Navy and mostly very young. We then had to get a small landing craft to Shetland, where our training base was to be. We started from Fort William and, passing through the Caledonian Canal, proceeded up the north-east coast of Scotland to Orkney.

The landing craft was built on the lines of a Yorkshire coble and powered by a Ford V8 engine. Off the coast of Caithness it suddenly stopped. A very active little Newfoundland Petty Officer called Hitchcock jumped over the side to clear a blockage under water. We were close on a lee shore and things did not look very nice. When we reached Scapa Flow, I reported myself to the Admiral Commanding Orkney and Shetland. I asked him if he would like to see the boat. He came, but when he saw my men, he said, "What are these?"— we were all wearing khaki battledress with naval caps and flashes. Then he said that he could not possibly have our boat going about on his sea without either wireless or recognition signals.

We were kept for a long time at Scapa; Christmas came and went, but still we were held up. "Red" Ryder came up to see if he could shift us, but he could not move the Admiral.

At last, I heard of an ML which was going to Shetland; I had a wire towing bridle made and at last we got away. The ML dropped us at Lerwick. We then proceeded to Balta Sound, in the extreme north of Shetland, under our own steam. There we met the rest of the party. We were an odd lot. The unit was commanded by Major Andrew Croft, an old friend of mine with much Arctic experience. Under him came Quintin Riley, an RNVR Officer who had been at my prep school, and Gino's expedition to Greenland. Christopher Dalgety and David Haig-Thomas were there, and also a gang of Canadian soldiers who were to teach us about canoes. In addition there were some Norwegian soldiers. By now it had been revealed that we were bound for Norway (which I did not consider the Arctic) and that there, we were supposed to live on an island and make a nuisance of ourselves to German ships.

As in Orkney, so in Shetland: it never stopped blowing gales. As soon as one from the south-west finished, another would start from the north-east. When I reached Balta Sound, I put the boat on a mooring and joined the others on a camping trip. I got back to find that the mooring had dragged and the boat was ashore. After fixing up rollers, skids and hauling ropes, we got all hands on to hauling her out. We patched her up temporarily and then I took her to Lerwick to be properly repaired.

We found kayaking very difficult in the broken water up there. David Haig-Thomas, a great expert in a kayak, was very nearly drowned one day. The weather, as well as the short days, made training so difficult that it was decreed we should move further south.

So we went to Loch Carron on the west coast of Scotland. Here it was much more peaceful, although it rained all the time. We had to train with weapons and gadgets that we had never seen before, Bren guns, grenades, walkie-talkie wireless sets, commando knives and canoes of various sorts. The Canadian experts insisted that the four men who made up a canoe crew should paddle kneeling up on the ribs. We found this hard on the knees.

One day when we were practising throwing live grenades, one of them did not go off although it had had its pin pulled out. We could not leave it lying about, so Andrew and I went to have a look at it. The spring had not come off and there was no knowing if the grenade would explode when touched. At length one of us seized it, his fingers over the spring. Soon the pin was back again and all was safe.

The War had never come to this out-of-the-way village. The people made a great fuss of our men, who were all billeted on them. If they got their feet wet when training, the villagers thought the officers had ill-treated them and talked about their "poor boys".

We had little transport of our own and used to hire a lorry to take our men to the hills for training. One Sunday we rang up the garage to ask for this lorry. The answer was that we couldn't have it because it was the Sabbath. We said we were quite aware of this but that there was a War on. The reply to that was "Oh! yes, we know that, but not *here*."

Kyle of Lochalsh was the Naval Base of minelayers. The railway there would not take passengers on a Sunday, so the only communication was by road, with a ferry across Loch Carron. This ferry also declined to work on Sundays. The Admiral at Kyle told the ferryman that he would take it over himself. The ferry went on working.

We used to practise going out in our kayaks and sticking limpet mines on the minelayers. Although the ships were alerted, we quite often stuck on our limpets undetected.

While we were doing this training, unknown to us a battle was raging at high level in Whitehall. We heard afterwards that the "crooked people" strongly objected to our interfering in Norway. Lord Mountbatten was all in favour of our doing something; nevertheless, the outcome was that the operation was off and we were disbanded. A few of the party, however, begged hard to be allowed to go. Permission was eventually granted, but not until the long days had come. The party, which included my Petty Officer Hiscock as well as the fine young Sub-Lieutenant Godwin, RNVR, were taken to Norway by MTB in May. They were dumped on an island which had been carefully chosen, and the MTB promised to come back for them in a fortnight's time. It did come back, but could find nobody. Afterwards, we heard that they had all been captured, taken to Sachsenhausen and killed. Hitler had said that he would not tolerate any more commandos.

*   *   *

My next job was collecting a landing-craft in America and bringing it over to Gibraltar. Since the Commanding Officers appointed to these landing-craft were not trained in deep water navigation, the idea was that "Ocean Commanding Officers" should bring them over.

A berth was found for me in the *Queen Mary* and I joined her on the Clyde. But there was a delay. A buzz went round the ship that we were held up for some VIP rumoured to be anybody from the Aga Khan downwards. A gang of carpenters came to make special doors on to aft deck; marine sentries were then posted there. We saw cases of champagne being loaded. We were driven out of the officers' quarters on aft deck and bundled below. The cabins we were allotted were the old two berth cabins of the ship and contained eighteen bunks each, troop quarters used to bring over the American troops.

At last a large number of people arrived. At the end came Winston Churchill. Then we sailed.

I ran into Hilary Saunders whom I had known in NID. This was a great comfort, for he was such very good company. Like myself, he was one of those deposed from aft deck and he invited me to share his cabin. He gave a lecture to the passengers on the Fall of France, at which he had been present.

It was unthinkable that Naval Officers should have a week with nothing to do. We were either made into submarine look-outs or appointed baggage officers. I chose the former and used to keep my watch on the bridge, which was over one hundred feet above the water. It took me fifteen minutes to climb up there from down below. But this was a fascinating job. I could see the escorting cruisers burying their bows in the sea to keep up with our speed; we were doing twenty-five knots. In the daytime members of the "Purdah party" including Lord Beaverbrook could be seen from the bridge, some of them reclining on the sun deck. Sometimes Winston would on the bridge, dressed in his well-known siren suit.

Another job we were given was to take charge of lifeboats in case of emergency. I drew number one boat on come the starboard side. It happened to be the one to which Winston and the First Sea Lord (Sir Dudley Pound) were allocated. I had visions of having a fascinating time with these two, listening to their stories and being given one of Winston's cigars.

At lifeboat drill, Winston did not appear, but a soldier in battledress turned up with a Tommy gun. I asked him who he was. He said he had come to look after Mr. Churchill. It appeared to me that, if he was in danger of capture by the enemy, Winston had arranged to have himself shot.

When we reached the other side we were met by an impressive squadron of American cruisers. Our VIPs were disembarked at Quebec, while we were all herded below.

Two of our passengers (not among the VIPs) were Lord and Lady Beveridge. After a time, Lady Beveridge was not to be seen. When he was asked why this was, her husband said that she had been bitten by bugs and could not appear in public.

We disembarked at New York, and the Naval officers were sent to the Barbizon Plaza Hotel. Here there was a wonderful hospitality organization. Whatever you said you would like to do, the attractive girl at the desk arranged. It was almost impossible to breathe in the streets of New York; there seemed to be no air at all, nothing but petrol fumes.

After a few days, I took passage by train to Norfolk, Virginia. It was a rather dirty journey with a great deal of grit blowing in. There I found my ship, which, in company with seventeen others, was to form a "flight" for the crossing. We were to be under the command of Alan Villiers, the great sailing-ship man. These landing-craft were fine ships. Of about three hundred tons, they could carry two hundred troops. They had eight engines joined together, in two banks of four; their speed was eighteen knots. In order not to strain the engines, Villiers proposed to make the passage at eleven knots, via Bermuda. The battleship *Queen Elizabeth* was in dock after her "incident" at Alexandria. An Italian motor boat, or midget submarine, had sneaked into the harbour to attach a squib on the bottom of both the *Valiant* and the *Queen Elizabeth*. The squibs went off and both ships sat on the bottom. An old friend of mine, Launcelot Fleming, now Bishop of Portsmouth, was Padre of the *Queen Elizabeth*. I dined with him on board his ship and heard of the anti-British feeling in America. Every time a window or a street lamp was broken, there were headlines in the papers saying "Atrocities by the British Navy". Nevertheless he had arranged that every man in the ship's company should take some leave in an American home. They were very popular.

One day when I was crossing the harbour from Portsmouth to Norfolk on the ferry boat, in uniform, of course, a man came up to me saying, "Are you a limey?" I replied that I was afraid I was. He said, "Waal! we don't want you here." I told him that I did not choose to come there but was sent. He answered, "Waal! we don't want you here anyway."

The passage home proceeded according to plan. We called at Bermuda, which was very pleasant, and carried on to Gibraltar along latitude thirty-two. It was good weather with a hot sun. When there was a sea, the ship, which was of welded construction, used to whip. Every day at noon we used to make our position by flags. By working things out beforehand, it was possible to hoist the signal within five minutes of noon.

After arrival at Gibraltar, where Quintin turned up for the night, we handed back the ships to their proper COs, and took passage for England in an antiquated liner.

*   *   *

After some leave, I was appointed to HMS *Garth*, a Hunt Class Destroyer based on Sheerness. We used to escort the east coast convoys and sometimes the Channel convoys.

One night, we were sent on an operation over to the French coast. We were to act as a decoy, tempting the German Air Force to come out in strength to attack us; our Air Force would then shoot them down. But the Jerries wouldn't play, so nothing happened.

We carried about nine officers and two hundred men. It was very interesting for me to see how the "real" Navy worked.

One trouble we had was that the RAF liked to practise diving on us out of the sun. We would never be quite certain whether the aeroplanes were ours or the enemy's. The Captain had to decide in about five seconds whether to open fire or not. After a time our ship was taken over by Captain "D". I was sent to take the damage control course in London and left the ship.

*   *   *

My next appointment was as First Lieutenant of the new Castle Class Corvette, *Tintagel Castle*, which was being built in Scotland. I had to go up to Troon to stand by while the job of construction was going on. When I got there, I found there was no accommodation; everywhere was full of "combined ops". The ship was only half built and not even a cat could sleep aboard her.

At last, I found a boarding house where the landlady said she would see me. When I went to be interviewed, she told me that all the other lodgers were elderly people and must not be disturbed; I was not to come in late at night; I was to clean my own shoes and do my own black-out. After I had been accused of gross carelessness in tearing the black-out curtain and poking the fire—which I had not realized was a crime—I found a nice hotel, where Mollie came up to join me.

My new Captain came up and we had a little office in the ship-yard. Here we set to work to plan the organization of the ship. We made out the Watch and Quarter Bill, and Action Stations and allotted jobs to the still absent crew.

At last the ship was completed. She was of about 1,600 tons, carrying a four-inch gun, a new anti-submarine weapon called the Squid, Oerlikon guns, depth charges, and the latest Asdic and Radar. She was a single screw ship driven by a steam engine. The crew joined from Devonport and were all berthed on board. Our complement was about six officers and one hundred and ten ratings.

At this time the Navy was "scraping the barrel" to find crews; moreover, the Chiefs' and Petty Officers' Mess at Devonport had been hit by a bomb, with heavy casualties. We were a Devonport ship, and most of the crew were Macs from Glasgow or Liverpool. They were largely conscripts who had only just joined the Navy. A number of them were quite uncivilized and did not even know how to use a knife and fork. They had never obeyed an order in their lives. On one occasion a very nice Leading Seaman told one of them to take off his cap in the Mess; the fellow promptly pulled out a knife.

The first thing we had to do was to go round to Tobermory, where we would be "worked up" by Admiral Stephenson. He had every destroyer, frigate and corvette that went into the Battle of the Atlantic through his hands from the beginning. On the way round nearly all the crew were seasick, men on the bridge standing there with a bucket beside them.

We were all in a great panic about this three weeks' "working up", my Captain (Lieutenant Atkinson, DSC, RNR), who had been there before, no less than anyone else. Admiral Stephenson had a fearsome reputation. It was said that, with a clever coxswain in his barge, he would sneak alongside at any time of the day or night and come aboard and create chaos. Sometimes he would demand that the entire crew should come ashore for drill. He had a direct line to the Admiralty and through this, it was said, he would contrive to have any officer he didn't like out of the ship. These he would put on his own Stall, and, when he considered them efficient, he would put them back on another ship. A current story had it that he once came aboard a Canadian ship and directly he had been saluted by the First Lieutenant, flung his cap to the deck saying "Incendiary bomb. Do something about it." Number One promptly kicked it over the side. The Admiral, undeterred, said, "Man overboard! Lower all boats and save him." His gold laced cap was retrieved.

The first thing that happened when we got to Tobermory, was a signal from the Admiral ordering us to send eighty men ashore for drill. We had to include most of our cooks and stewards to make up this number, but we knew that if we sent only seventy-nine there would be trouble.

The Admiral lived in a ship called HMS *Western Isles*. Every Captain was asked to dine and every First Lieutenant to lunch with him. Every day, classes of officers and men went to the *Western Isles* to have training in Asdic and other things. When we went to sea for exercises, the Admiral was always there to see what happened. At times there were pulling races in our whalers; I found that the best crew were the stokers.

The most dreaded thing about all this was the final inspection. If the ship did not pass, she was kept there another fortnight. We were lucky: The Admiral was having heart trouble and a Captain did our inspection. So instead of having to do extraordinary things, such as hoisting depth charges to the bridge, we had a very peaceful time. He passed us fit for battle. We then went to join our Escort Group at Greenock.

Our first convoy was a slow one to escort to Newfoundland. The escorts all had appointed stations round it, and our speed of advance was supposed to be six and a half knots, but in bad weather we hardly moved. We ourselves zig-zagged at twelve to fifteen knots. When, after several weeks, we reached St. Johns, we got a very pleasant consignment of fruit juice from the Canadians. Our coxswain, a fine old Petty Officer, had a fit there, but he soon recovered. It was not long before it was time to take another convoy back and again we made the slow traipse home. We had the usual trouble with stragglers, but by this time the U Boats were almost dead, so we had no interference from them.

One morning during the voyage, the Chief Bos'n's mate, the "Buffer", came into my cabin in a state of alarm to say that the cat was missing. I told him to look under my bunk. Sure enough, there was the cat, with her kittens, in my boot locker. My Captain passed the signal round the group, "First Lieutenant and kittens all doing well." Unfortunately, the next time we sailed from Greenock, the cat got left ashore; her three kittens were reared by the Chief Bos'n's mate on tinned milk.

After a voyage of several weeks we reached the Clyde at last and went to Glasgow for a refit and the installation of some new gadgets.

Our next convoy was a so-called fast one (twelve knots) to Gibraltar. We were to carry the Senior Officer of the Group, a Commander RN, and his staff. I had the job of fixing up their accommodation while my Captain was on leave.

We had an uneventful trip, being routed well out into the Atlantic. While we were at sea we heard the first news of D Day and I had to give a lecture to the hands. Knowing nothing about my subject, I based my remarks on the words of Shakespeare's *Henry V*, who had followed the same route through Normandy.

The Commodore of the convoy sometimes used to make emergency turns; these the Merchant ships executed as if they were a Naval Squadron.

Before we got to Gibraltar, the Senior Officer passed a signal round the group that every ship was to provide a feature in a concert to be given when we got to Gibraltar. Our turn, I remember, was called "Up Spirits".

We returned to Londonderry. I rang up Mollie to hear news of home. She was just starting to tell me there had been some trouble, when we were cut off; apparently you were not allowed to speak of trouble on the telephone. What had actually happened was that a flying bomb had hit a tree about a quarter of a mile from the house and broken all the windows.

*   *   *

I was next appointed as a Watch Keeping Officer to the *Agamemnon*, a blue funnel liner of about eight thousand tons. She had been taken over by the Navy, converted to a mine layer and was based at Kyle of Lochalsh. She was one of the ships on which we had practised sticking limpets from kayaks while in the Arctic Commando.

Now she was to be sent to Vancouver to be converted into a beer ship. The American Navy had a fleet train in which there was a number of ice-cream ships. Their Lordships, in their wisdom, had decided that, for the War in the Pacific, we should have beer ships.

When I joined at Kyle, my new Captain, who was a very nice Commander RN, told me that he would like me to be the navigator. I asked permission, which was granted, to go home to get my sextant. On returning, however, I found a very superior navigator installed Lieutenant Commander RNR from the *Dryad* (The Navigation School).

Having called at the Clyde for repairs we sailed again, in company with a sister ship, for the Panama Canal. The ship was run Merchant Service fashion, having an RNR First Lieutenant. We kept standing watches, which is to say that we were always on watch at the same time day and night. I kept the middle watch from midnight till four a.m. and, in the daytime, both dog watches, for five weeks. We zig-zagged across the Atlantic at fifteen knots. I remember that one night, during my watch, I saw the other ship, to starboard, bearing down on us; I promptly ordered hard aport. They had forgotten the zig-zag.

When we were half way over, there was a slight flap; it was discovered that the fore-peak was full of water which could not be pumped out. It seemed that we might have to put into Bermuda; however, a hole was made in the watertight bulkhead to let out the water into the bilge.

One day, for some reason, I rang down "Stop engines." In two minutes the chief was on the bridge. "What are you doing with my engines?" he shouted. I said, "Nothing, only stopped them." He went off the bridge muttering, "You've spoilt my revs."

When we reached Cristobal, where we were to enter the Panama Canal, most of the crew went ashore. I was made the Officer of the Day to receive the drunks and had to put one man in the cells.

After passing through the Canal, we sailed up the west coast to Victoria, near Vancouver, arriving on Christmas Eve. Nobody knew we were coming. In spite of this there was a Christmas party for every man in both ships' companies.

I returned overland, *via* Canadian Pacific and New York. Having spent a week there, awaiting passage, I was given a berth in HMS *Nelson*, which had been doing a refit in the States. She had just been fitted with a marvellous new gadget called Loran, with which it was possible to find our position by wireless in the middle of the Atlantic. On entering Portsmouth, I thought I would go on the bridge to see the fun. All the Hierarchy, in due order, was up there: the Captain, the principal Control Officer, the Officer of the Watch, the Midshipman of the Watch, the Petty Officer of the Watch and the Navigator. There was a dead silence only broken by the clicking of the gyro-compass. Eventually a sea-gull flew by. "Pilot, is that an albatross?" asked the Captain. The Navigator looked at it through his binoculars and said, "I'm afraid I don't know, Sir." "Oh!" said the Captain. Silence was resumed and only the compass went on clicking.

After this it was the end of the War as far as I was concerned. The remaining job was the disarmament of the Germans in Denmark. After a course in London, at the time of the rockets, I found myself as First Lieutenant of the Naval Party training a batch of sailors at Plymouth.

During the time I was there, VE Day was celebrated. The sailors had a great party on the Hoe and made a splendid fire of all the deck-chairs. The Fire Brigade arrived and the sailors turned the hoses on the firemen.

After a passage from Rosyth to Copenhagen in landing. craft, we settled down to a good time in Denmark. The person I chiefly remember was our Padre, Arthur Watson. He was, and still is, a dear and great friend.

There they tried to make me into a Lieutenant Commander. I told the Admiral's Secretary that I would rather not, as it would be such a bother to change my uniform.

VJ Day arrived and so did my demob. Thus ended my six years with the Wavy Navy. I think I must have been the senior Lieutenant in the Navy List.

August Courtauld as navigator.

August with his son Stephen Courtauld, born at Spencers 9th September 1940.

17

Spencers

WE MOVED to Spencers, Great Yeldham, in the September of 1937. Our third child, Julien, was born there on January 1st.

We have six children now, all born at home except the last, who made her appearance in the middle of a summer holiday. The eldest, Perina, is twenty-four, our first son, Christopher, twenty-one and studying at Trinity College, Cambridge. Then come the other boys: Julien, whom I have just mentioned, Stephen and William. The first is doing military service—Stephen is at Public School and William about to go there. Our second daughter, Susie, is six. There does not seem to be anything particularly wrong with any of them up of them up to the present—and indeed there should not be, for Mollie brought up her children beautifully. Her love for them has always seemed to me a wonderful thing. Throughout the twenty-five years of our married life, she has helped me, too, in all my various doings and been my mate and standby.

Our home is a plain Georgian house, sunny and pleasant, which was built about 1750 by the grand-daughter of the Great Duke of Marlborough (Viscountess Bateman) We have painted on the bedroom doors the names of Marlborough's battles—Blenheim, Ramillies, Oudenarde, Malplaquet. Spencers attracted us also by its fine trees and old walled garden. In the little park there is a splendid pollard oak. Queen Elizabeth put a tax on unpollarded oaks so that timbers should be produced for building her ships; our tree is supposed to date from that time. There is enough room for four people to sit in the fork, and we often used to climb up there to have tea. It takes five people with their arms outstretched to span the trunk. Sometimes we would sleep out on the lawn under the cedars or the lime tree, liking to hear the whisper of the trees in the quiet night and to see the old familiar stars wheel back.

I had a mare called Pancake on which I sometimes used to hunt. She had a foal which we called "Mac 2" after my first command in the Navy. Between October and January, I used to get in a certain amount of shooting.

When John Rymill's expedition returned, we were given a husky bitch called Maureen. She was an attractive creature but, before she could have puppies, she picked up a poisoned rat, and we were unable to save her. Mollie gave me a young labrador bitch, Tangle, when I came home from the war. Tangle was the daughter of a rather famous retriever in Essex—Jess, belonging to Colonel J. O. Parker of Faulkbourne. Although, I cannot say she was well trained, Tangle was a splendid retriever with the best nose of any dog I have ever known. She became a very dear friend, especially to the children. Eventually she married a fine dog with a good pedigree, who belonged to Colonel Cooper of Bulmer. She had two official litters of pups by her husband and one unofficial family, by whom I don't know. At present we have one pup from each of the official litters—Duchess, a bitch from the first litter, and Gladwin, a dog from the second. The unofficial pups were raffled at a fête. Tangle used to bring her pups to play on the lawn, where they were a very pretty sight. Both our present dogs have their mother's nose and they retrieve well. Gladwin, a big, handsome dog, has been properly trained; Duchess is a house dog and has been rather spoiled. The only dog pup of the first litter was taken by Colonel Cooper, as was his right, and it has been given the name of Spencer.

At the time of Gino's expedition, my sister Betty was married to Ralph Rayner. The wedding was at Halstead Church where, twenty-five years later, my daughter Perina was married. Rayner was an officer of the Royal Signals and acted as our secretary when we were away in Greenland on the expedition. Later, he became MP for the Totnes Division, Devon. Guy Wreford-Brown and I went down there to help him in and spent our time driving over the moors in the old Lagonda. He remained a Member for the next twenty years, always with a good majority, and still lives in the West Country in the house which he and Betty built on the hill behind Dawlish.

My father-in-law and I were very keen on fires. One day we heard that Wethersfield Manor, the home of Sir Fortesque Flannery, was ablaze, and rushed over at once. We found the whole house well alight and the Fire Brigade looking elegant on the lawn. Lady Flannery, in tears, was sitting on a chair in the stable yard, wearing all her jewellery and being comforted by her women. We two got on the roof and, having asked the Fire Brigade to send us up a hose, had great fun drenching the undamaged wing. Finally, half the house was burnt down.

Jamie Scott and I once went for a walking tour in Scotland, going to the west coast *via* Loch Moidart. Walking up the great sea-loch of Loch Nevis, we reached Sgurrna Ciche, and put up at a little croft at the foot of it. Here the old couple insisted on giving us their bed as, they said, the cow would calve that night. They fed us beautifully, with true Scottish hospitality, and when we left next morning refused to take a penny in payment. We had a very different experience another day when we called at a house to get some food—we had had nothing since breakfast and it was about thirty miles before we would reach anywhere else. Seeing some hens about the place, we asked the man with a black beard who came to the door if he had any eggs. "The hens are no laying the day," said he. We then asked for some bread. He told us there wasn't any. We asked how far it was to the next house where we might get some. "I dinna ken," he answered. Having been successfully repelled, we walked on.

The summer of 1939 was lovely. On returning from Norway, in *Duet*, we sat on the lawn, listening to the War starting up on the wireless. When the bombing began. we could see the glare in the sky over London from our windows. Spencers has a good, old-fashioned brick arched cellar; here the children used to sleep. Most of the house was shut up, and we fed in the hall by the front door. The drawing room was a clothing dump for the WVS, in which Mollie took a leading part. She was local Honorary Secretary of the Soldiers', Sailors' and Airmen's Families Association

One night, when she was in her bath, an enemy plane came over to drop a stick of bombs. One landed on the lawn, and as she jumped out of the bath, the window fell into it. Eventually the police and air wardens turned up. They insisted on going out in the dark to see where this bomb had dropped, and fell into the crater. Later we planted a chestnut tree in it.

Towards the end of the War, when I was again away on service, Mollie had a hunch that something would happen. In spite of Nannie's protests, the children were taken down into the cellar once again. During the night the warning went, and Mollie, going to the front door, saw a flying bomb coming up the drive. It hit a tree, completely flattening two small houses. Once more all the windows came in and the children's beds were covered in broken glass. Their being in the cellar could only have been the hand of Providence.

In the summer of 1940, our fourth child, Stephen was born, and when he was a month old, Mollie brought him down to see me at HMS *Hornet*, Gosport. When she arrived at the station, a raid started, everyone was herded into a shelter, and there Mollie had to feed the child. Later, when she was on her way to come over to the *Hornet*, another raid started at Lee and she had to get into a ditch. And when she finally reached the *Hornet*, I was aboard my MTB; she was pushed down into the shelter with the WRNS.

While I was on my way across the Atlantic in 1943, our fifth child, William, was born at Spencers.

Coming back to my own country when the war was over, I naturally could not help collecting committees. I was made chairman of the Essex Rural Community Council, which I survived for fifteen years, and of the Essex Association of Boys' Clubs, where I still function, On my return in September 1945, it was suggested that I put up for the Essex County Council. It was only a By-Election, due to a neighbour becoming an Alderman, and I was elected unopposed. At the proper election the following year, again I got in unopposed for the Belchamp and Bumpstead Division.

I found the County Council meant endless Committees. There were also the Divisional Educational Executive and the Colchester Group Hospital Committees, both of which I had been put on. Personally, I have now come to the conclusion that all committees are a waste of time and have resigned from the lot, except the Lifeboat Committee and the Essex Association of Boys' Clubs.

Before the war, I had been put on the Council of the Royal Geographical Society; after the war, I was made one of the two honorary secretaries. I was also on the Committee of the Scott Polar Research Institute at Cambridge and on the Council of the Cruising Association.

One day, somebody rang up to say that my name was being put up for Deputy Lieutenant. "Oh Lord," I thought, "this isn't my cup of tea at all," and asked him to get it stopped. He said it was too late; my name had gone up to the King. Accordingly, I was made a DL in 1946.

That summer we went to Champéry in Switzerland, near the French border, and did a bit of climbing there with the children, Chris, then aged eleven, and I were on our way down the hills one day when we got caught in a thunderstorm. We found ourselves at the top of some cliffs which we could not get down: the only thing possible was to climb to the summit again. Then we had to descend by the way we had originally gone up to the top, and it was dark by the time we reached the valley.

August, Perina, Julien and Mollie Courtauld in the Alps.

The following summer we took a house at Acharacle. I sailed *Duet* via Holland to Loch Moidart, which was within walking distance of the house. It is the place where Bonnie Prince Charlie landed in 1745. That summer of 1947 was incredibly fine and hot on the west coast of Scotland. The boys had a wonderful time bathing, climbing and sailing. One day we sailed to the Island of Eigg, where a friend of ours was living. On the way back, as we were entering Loch Moidart, which is unlighted, we went on a rock in the darkness. We floated off all right, however, when the tide rose. It was on this trip, and on his thirteenth birthday, that Chris developed polio.

Mollie had a pretty tough time for the next two years; much of the time Chris was at home lashed up in plaster. He could only move his hands and arms, but he never complained. There were tutors, physio-therapists and doctors—nineteen doctors before a surgeon, Professor Seddon, produced the answer. After Chris had been in plaster a long time, Seddon performed an operation which he told us would be the most severe thing known in surgery. It took him and another surgeon four and a half hours; at the end of them, Professor Seddon was completely whacked. When he rang me up in the middle of the night, I could tell despite his guarded tones that things were not too good. Next day, Sister told us Christopher had had a collapse from shock. Seddon had stayed with him all night and Chris's life had only been saved by immediate action; Sister said later that she had thought Chris was gone.

It was Professor Seddon who recommended the warm-water swimming for Chris which prompted us to borrow Ian Fleming's house in Jamaica. Our intended trip in *Duet* having failed, we took passage in the Cunarder *Media* for New York. It was December, the weather was bad, and we were several days late. From New York we flew to Jamaica *via* Florida. Looking all over the island and swimming in Ian Fleming's lagoon gave us a wonderful time. We wore face masks with a breathing tube up to the surface; with these we could see the beautifully coloured fish and, sometimes, on the edge of the reef, real monsters.

We met some very pleasant Americans who came over to Jamaica every year. In particular there was Mrs. Melhado and Mr. and Mrs. Woolsey, who have remained our friends. When the time came to return, we sailed in the same ship, the *Media*.

As a thank offering for my release from the Greenland ice cap and Christopher's deliverance from polio, we thought we'd like to put some panelling in St. Andrew's Church at Great Yeldham. The East end of the Church was panelled in oak to a design by our old friends Paul Paget and John Seely (now Lord Mottistone), and the work was carried out by those fine craftsmen, the brothers Mabbitt of Colchester. At the dedication service by the Bishop of Chelmsford, Christopher read the lesson.

About this time I was put on the Committee of Management of the Royal National Lifeboat Institution. Here I worked with a fine team of men and found it all fascinating.

Our next holiday abroad was in Spain, where we thought we would like to have a look at the pictures and old towns. We took our car, going by Chartres, where we inspected the stained glass through' binoculars, and we took in a visit to the Île d'Oléron, where my Huguenot ancestors had lived before they escaped to England in 1689. It is a charming island, which grows its own wine and has a splendid beach facing the Atlantic. Hunting round for family relics, we came across an old woman working in the fields. "Have you ever heard of anyone called Courtauld?" we asked her. "Oh yes," she replied, "I can tell you all about them." "That's very interesting," we said. "Do tell us." "They were all pirates, the whole lot of them," said she.

Of the lovely old towns in Spain, we liked Segovia and Toledo best. We stayed a few days in Madrid, where we spent most of the time in the Prado looking at the pictures, which we thought the finest collection we had ever seen. What specially impressed us were the El Grecos, not only there but also in Toledo and in various churches. We had an introduction to the late Duke of Alba and lunched with him, finding him most charming. He let us see his collection of treasures, among them personal letters from Queen Elizabeth to his ancestor who commanded the Army which had driven the Moors out of Spain. There was a remarkable statue of this early Duke of Alba standing in full armour prodding down with a spear at three dragons which surrounded him. One of these dragons had the face of Queen Elizabeth and another the face of the Pope.

At a monastery we were shown some clothing which had been worn by a former Queen of Spain, sister of the Black Prince, who had come out to Spain as a young girl after her marriage.

We returned over the Pyrenees, stopping on the way home in Périgeux. There we saw the famous caves of Lescaux, with their wonderful thirty thousand year old drawings of wild animals.

In August 1950 our sixth child, Susie, was born, completing the family.

The following year my mother died at The Howe. My father decided to sell the lease of the family house in Palace Green, which has now become the private residence of the Dutch Ambassador. The following spring, Betty, Peter and I thought we would throw a party before the house passed out of the hands of the family. All our friends came and it was a great success.

In 1953 my father died, aged eighty-seven. His estate of about two thousand acres, part at Halstead and part at Blackmore End, now became mine, and it was something of a problem to know how to deal with it. I appointed a very good agent in Alan Nott; with his help and the great experience and kindness of my father's solicitor, Sir Leslie Farrer, KCVO, we have managed. To begin with, I wanted to keep on the men who had worked at The Howe, some of whom had been there since I was a boy. So we turned the place into a market garden; it produced plenty of stuff, but there was nowhere to sell it. We thought of going to live at The Howe and putting Spencers on the market. But even with the help of a big firm of London agents, as well as that of a country firm, only three people came to look at the place, and none of them even nibbled. We are now very glad they didn't.

The Howe has been sold, although it was considered unsaleable. Unwanted properties have been dealt with and farm rents have been raised from the ten shillings per acre that my father got to a more reasonable figure.

In 1952, one of the tenant farmers died. We decided to take on his farm—Summer's Hall, at Blackmore End. I was fearful about doing this as I know nothing about farming. Alan Nott, however, said he could manage it for me, which he does, most excellently. This farm has given me much pleasure during the last few years. It is of four hundred acres, mostly good land. I was surprised that all the original men signed on with me, for it was to be expected that they would find better jobs elsewhere. There were ten of them, mostly elderly but experts in their way. It is a good thing to have this farm for any of the boys who may want it in the future. We had to cart from scratch, giving it a complete outfit of new equipment. We have tractors, a combine harvester, potato spinner, beet spinner, sprayer and corn dressing plant; all are diesel driven, except the corn dresser, which is electric. We grow wheat, barley, oats, peas, beans and sugar beet. We fatten bullocks, sheep and pigs, and we rear a number of calves on two nurse cows. Eventually, out of these, we hope to raise a pedigree herd of shorthorns. We also make a good quantity of hay as well as harvesting Cocksfoot grass seed.

We have appointed a farm foreman, John Taylor, who is in charge. Unfortunately, soon after joining us, he was brushing a hedge and got a twig in his eye. The eye had to be taken out, but he seems to get on just as well without it. Under his leadership they are a fine team of men.

Two interesting men used to live at Summer's Hall. One was Adrian Pelly, who now manages the Queen's farm at Windsor. He came, a good many years ago, to learn his farming here at Blackmore End. The other was Uncle George, the eldest son of my grandfather. When I was a boy he lived at The Waver, which is now the foreman's house. He tried many different religions, including Buddhism, before ending up as a Roman Catholic. It was said he lived there so as to be more than seven miles from a Roman Catholic Church, which meant that he would be excused from going to Mass. He was a recluse and a bit of a mathematician. When my father had a problem he used to send it to him; he always solved it. I remember one which bothered my father and which I asked my maths master at school to explain. He couldn't do it. Uncle George, however, produced many pages of explanation; but as neither my father nor anyone else could understand it, it was not of much help. The problem was to understand how a cunning way of multiplication worked. You halved the lower figure until you reached the figure one, omitting the halves. You then doubled the other figure the same number of times. You crossed out the figures in the second column opposite an even number in the first. The sum of what remained in the second column was the answer. Here is an example of it:

9 multiplied by	10
4	20
2	40
1	80
Answer	90

In the County Council election of 1949 I was opposed by a woman. My Division was the largest area in the County but one of the smallest in population. My cousin Sydney Butler (Mrs. R. A. Butler) came round the twenty-six villages with me. We had a loud speaker on the car, but few came to hear us in the cold and dark of an early April night. We could also play music. We had two records "Buttons and Bows" and the "Eton Boating Song". At last Sydney said, "If you play that song once more I shall send all my sons to Harrow."

I felt better being an elected member of the Council, rather than getting in unopposed. At the Council meetings I used to find and raise something in small print on a back page. Sometimes the Press described the result as an "uproar".

At the next election, in 1952, I was again opposed, this time by a man in Yeldham. Not considering that my opponent had much chance, I did not do a campaign at all. The result was the same, and I found myself sentenced to another three years. In this Council the Socialists had control. I have great admiration for the man who was then Chairman of the Council; Mr. William Bennett.

The Divisions of the County were then rearranged and mine was abolished. I did not stand again in 1955. I made the following little "good-bye" speech at my last meeting of the Council:

"I would like to pay my tribute to the many friends I have found on the Council during my ten years of service. I have found during these years many good men and women sitting on both sides of the Chamber who are devoted to the work and who spend their lives untiringly in the service of Essex. I shall miss them and I shall miss, too, the Officers of the Council. They have helped me many times, always with courtesy and always cheerfully.

"In particular I would express my admiration for that great man of Essex, our Chairman. Although, unfortunately, he and I did not sit on the same side, we always pulled together and, since he has been our Chairman, I have received the greatest kindness from him always. I admire his qualities as a leader of men, as well as his unflagging zeal to promote the well-being of the people of Essex.

"No considerations of party, of distance or of the hours of weariness, drive him from his course which lies straight, directed to the truth and to what is good. May he be an example to us all in doing the best for our beloved County.

"And what a County! There is no doubt that it is the best county in Britain. If you want a piece of land ploughed, where will you find a better ploughman? If you want to build a boat, where will you find a better builder or a better man to sail her? If you want to have a piece of lovely material made, where will you find better weavers than in Essex? Have we not at Chelmsford three of the foremost industries of the country? One started by a man who began life as a midshipman in the Crimean War and who, after a distinguished career in the Army, settled down here to perfect the dynamo, the machine which took electricity out of the experimental stage of stroking the cat, to the practical uses which we know today. Then there was the invention of wireless telegraphy which, made by an Italian, was entirely developed by Essex men who founded here the firm of world renown. The third is the famous firm of ball bearing makers. Where our Spitfires would have been without them we shudder to think.

"Luckily we 'keeps ourselves to ourselves'. If we didn't Hitler might have heard about us and then nothing might have been left of Chelmsford or the hall in which we sit.

"In conclusion, here are the words of Chesterton:

'Smile at us, pay us, pass us;
But do not quite forget
We are the people of England
And we have not spoken yet.' "

August Courtauld (left) haymaking with Charlie Palmer (right).

I had to take my turn as High Sheriff, following my father and grandfather, in 1953. I was much alarmed at the prospect and would have got out of it if I could. My term came just after my father died. I found, however, that, with the wonderful experience and ability of my under sheriff, A. D. P. Thomson, it was all quite easy. My first duty was to attend the Memorial Service of Queen Mary in Chelmsford Cathedral. There was something of a panic to get a top hat in time, but it all passed off all right in the end. The Judges were most charming and all difficulties were smoothed aside by Thomson. In court I used to sit on the right of the Judge in the uniform of a Deputy Lieutenant. Next to me came my Chaplain, the Reverend A. W. Swallow of Halstead, then Mollie and after her, Thomson (in Court dress). Some of the trials were most interesting. There seems to be a lot of crime in Essex: we had three murders. One man was sentenced to death and we had to hang him. I did not go to the execution.

At each Assize we asked the Judges to dine. This was a somewhat formidable matter. One had to be on the doorstep to meet them and they had to go in to dinner in front of the ladies. However, like most of my duties as sheriff, these dinners seemed to pass off very well.

My year of office was that of the Coronation. At first we were told that there would be no room for the Sheriffs, though they had been invited to the Coronations of their Sovereigns from about the time of William the Conqueror. I believe a bit of a fuss was made behind the scenes; in any event, the Earl Marshal finally found room for us. A panic ensued to get suitable garb for the ceremony. Moss Brothers said that my father's scarlet DL's uniform could not be altered for me, so I decided to wear my father's Court dress. On the way to the Abbey at six a.m. we saw a poster which said "Everest climbed".

When, at last, we reached the Abbey, we were shown into some very good seats in the aisle just below the Screen. The point of the scabbard of my Dress sword had come off; the first thing that happened when I sat down was that the point of the sword stabbed the foot of the Sheriff next me. We had expected the four hours of waiting, before the service began, to be tedious, but they weren't. There was a continual procession up the aisle of notables in their robes. At last the Queen came, looking quite lovely. Her procession was magnificent. The music was very fine, as everybody knows. We could not see the Crowning itself, the Screen being in the way, but when the Queen came down the aisle wearing her crown, she looked wonderful. It was an occasion I shall never forget.

Later in the summer we had to give the usual garden party. The list of guests was laid down by tradition. There were about four hundred. Then, just as the Lord Lieutenant drove up, down came an almighty storm, and everybody had to shelter in the tea tent.

All the Mayors of Essex (and there are a good many) asked us to their receptions. We only went to two, those of the Mayor of West Ham (who is the senior Mayor in the county) and the Mayor of Chelmsford. At the latter, there were thirteen set speeches; I had to open the batting.

Before the war, I had the idea that there ought to be an anthology of Polar books. Many of these books are massive and there is a great number of them. It was arranged between two others and myself that we would divide up the material and each make extracts from his quota of books. After doing quite a lot, I discovered that the other two had done nothing about it. During the war I forgot the whole thing, but, going through my desk later, I found my old extracts. When I came to look at them again, I thought they were too good to lose. So I decided I would try to tackle the whole job myself and wrote to the Oxford University Press asking if they would be interested in publishing such an anthology. Mr. Cumberlege replied that they might. Polar exploration covers three thousand years of history; some of the writing about it is very fine.

I propose that the book—if it ever gets done—should be called *From the Ends of the Earth*.

Using a legacy left me by my mother, I decided to give a lifeboat to be stationed in Essex or Kent. I discovered that the Walton and Frinton Station was due for a new boat; the Duchess of Kent, President of the Institution, named her *Edian Courtauld* after my mother. This was one of the few fine days in the vile summer of 1954 and a lot of people came to Walton-on-the-Naze for the christening, which went off very well. The Duchess was, as always, completely charming.

In the middle of 1954 I got a letter from the Secretary of the Lifeboat Institution telling me he was much disturbed because the Standing Joint Committee of the Essex County Council had written to say they proposed to abolish, every alternate year, our Lifeboat Day in Essex. Could I do anything to help, he asked. So I wrote the following letter to every member of the Committee, having found out first what it was to which the Flag Day Committee, who were responsible, were making objection.

Trafalgar Day, 1954

Spencers, Gt. Yeldham, Essex

"Dear ...

I am writing to you on the subject of the Standing Joint Committee's decision to do away with Lifeboat Day every other year. The Committee of Management of the Institution, of which I am a member, are much concerned that this step should have been taken by such a great County as Essex.

"After I had been asked to enquire into this, I saw the Chairman of the Sub-Committee concerned, who told me that two of the chief reasons for the Committee taking this decision were:

1. That the Collectors were unpaid, overworked and tired of it.
2. That the Lifeboats collected salvage and that they should not therefore be supported by public contribution.

"I have promised to give the Chairman information on both these matters and on any others connected with the running of the Institution. In the meantime, I have made enquiries and cannot find any lack of enthusiasm among either the collectors, or the public, for Lifeboat Day. On the contrary, within the last few days two Honorary Secretaries of local branches have separately informed me that they consider that their branches would be destroyed by having to wait two years for Lifeboat Day. On our Day this summer, over two thousand pounds was collected in Essex, and I have had no complaint from anybody about the way in which this was done, or any resentment on the part of the public.

"On the question of Salvage, I would like to point out that this is a matter of a bargain between the Coxswain of the Lifeboat and the Master of the vessel in distress. It has nothing to do with the Institution, but if salvage is claimed the Institution do not pay rewards. The Laws of Salvage go back many centuries in the maritime history of our country. Our Lifeboats are maintained for saving life at sea, but if they should be successful also in saving a vessel from a position of danger, you might agree that it would be most unfair if they were denied the right to claim on the Insurance of the vessel where the crew of, say a tug, would do so. In fact Property Salvage Claims have very much reduced in recent years, and in the case of all Lifeboats it is a rare, and in some, an unknown event, for a Salvage Case to arise. Personally, after over thirty years of boating round the coasts of Britain, I have never had a Salvage Claim from any of our Lifeboats, though on many occasions I have been offered assistance by them.

"I am sure you will agree that it is essential for our Lifeboat Service to be kept efficient. I am confident that it is so, due to the devoted service of our Officers and the unselfish zeal of our crews. To run the Service at present costs about three-quarters of a million pounds a year. A great part of this income is derived from the small contributions spread over the whole of Great Britain and Ireland, given by the general public. To take away Lifeboat Day would not only remove this source of income but take away the interest and enthusiasm of the people.

"As an Essex man, I am most grieved that our county, with its dangerous sea-board and its three splendid Lifeboat Stations, should have taken such a decision. I can only say that I mean to do everything in my power to persuade you to reverse this decision.

"I would be most reluctant to do anything which would discredit your Committee, of which my father was Chairman for twenty years, but I think I should inform you that I have been assured the backing of the Press, who have promised to make this matter public when I give the word.

"I hope you will forgive my interference in your affairs.

Yours sincerely,

"To the Members of the Standing Joint Committee.

"Copies to: The Lord Lieutenant of Essex.
The High Sheriff of Essex.
The Chief Constable.
The Secretary RNLI.
The Clerk to the County Council."

At their December meeting, the Standing Joint Committee reversed its decision, so we got back our annual Lifeboat Day.

In January, my old friend, Francis Rennell invited Chris and me to accompany him to Australia. Being somewhat crippled with neuritis and having perforce given up most of my activities, there was nothing to prevent my going, and Chris got leave from Cambridge.

We sailed in January 1955 in the new P & O ship *Arcadia*, from Tilbury, in a thick fog. You could not see across the dock, but, with the aid of two Radars, we steamed down the river, dead slow. All the other ships were brought up to an anchor.

The *Arcadia* is a wonderful ship of about thirty thousand tons. She had been built with stabilizers and with the help of these she never rolled at all, although we had a heavy gale in the Indian Ocean.

When we got to Adelaide, we took an aeroplane to Penola, to stay with my old friend John Rymill (a member of Gino's expedition) at his family's sheep station, hallway between Adelaide and Melbourne. There Chris went out shooting with a rifle. He brought home some of the bag—opossum, wallaby, cockatoo, and kangaroo. One of the kangaroos was a "Forester" which measured seven feet from nose to tail; it was about the biggest ever shot on the station. I have now a belt, a watch-strap and a jacket made from the skin of this animal. It is very light, strong leather and entirely wind proof. We saw some of John's ten thousand sheep as well as his horses, which were beautiful Arabs. We went to another part of the station where he and some others had made a syndicate to clear the bush so as to grow strawberry clover seed. In spite of the official government pronouncement that this land could never be any good, we saw a very fine crop being harvested by eight combines. The seed is in great demand all over the world, as it is the only grass that will grow in a dry country. It is worth £1 a lb. and the crop we saw, grown on fifteen hundred acres, was likely to be worth £70,000.

We rejoined the ship at Melbourne, Chris carrying his kangaroo tail up the gangway. We had asked some people to dine with us on board and sent the tail to the galley to be cooked for dinner. A message came back that this could not be done, for it would take the whole afternoon to draw the sinews. We told them to use a bit more strength. We got our kangaroo tail, cooked like ox-tail for dinner; it was delicious. Our guests were all Australians but only one had ever tasted kangaroo before.

We went for tea with the Governor at his wonderful palace in Melbourne. He showed us some of it, including the ballroom, a foot longer than that at Buckingham Palace, and the state dining-room where fifty-four people can sit at table. The table in itself is very well worth seeing; it is a magnificent piece of Australian wood about sixty feet long. The Governor told us about the Great Ball given when the Queen was staying with him, and how, when she mounted the dais and turned, looking quite lovely, all the people in the great Ballroom sang the National Anthem.

We sailed that night for Sydney, where the last Test Match was on; Chris went to see it. Then, in order to get a little cooler, we flew to Canberra.

There we went to a great lunch party with the Governor General, Field Marshal Sir William Slim. It was very regal but quite delightful. Field Marshal Slim is a great chap and very popular all over Australia. We heard that he had lately been on a tour to the Northern Territory where the men consider themselves pretty tough. Sir William went into a low dive to see something of the people. He found a tough looking Northerner dressed in a bush shirt, foot-long spurs and a ten gallon hat, reading a comic paper. Suddenly, he looked up and saw the Field Marshal coming through the door, in full uniform with his medals. "Jesus Christ!" said the Northerner. "No, not quite. Only the Governor General," replied His Excellency.

After a visit to Courtauld's factory about eighty miles north of Sydney, it was time for me to return. I flew back in three days; we came down only to refuel. The one night's stop we had planned at Singapore had to be cancelled as we had been delayed. I had been told that this flight was very exhausting; I did not find it so, only boring. I had great admiration for the way the plane was run, and especially for the navigation. We flew right across the middle of Arabia, the Navigator taking star sights every hour.

Chris stayed in Australia for another four months. His tutor had written to say that, as he was taking one term off, he might as well have two, since he would have to do a fourth year anyway. He had a splendid time seeing the country, taking a lot of fine colour photographs and staying with various people we had met—in particular the Rothes in Sydney. He went to see the great Snowy Mountains Scheme which was being built up in the Australian Alps. He did a trek with a Padre who was looking after the Inland Mission, out into the middle of Queensland. They went as far as it was possible to go without getting bogged in a wide desert. He spent Easter with the Governor General at Government House. He returned to join me on my way to the Mediterranean in *Duet*.

In May of 1955 we decided to give a show of the Courtauld Silver at Spencers, in aid of the Friends of Essex Churches. In the eighteenth century my family had been silversmiths. The first of these was Augustine, who entered his mark in 1708. Then came Samuel, his son, followed by Louisa Perina. Their work is now highly regarded. We borrowed the silver from wherever we could trace it. The Lord Mayor of London lent a fine State Salt from the Mansion House. I have a number of pieces which my father gave me. The collection made a brave show when it was all arranged in two rooms by Mrs. Charles Round. It was open to public view on a Saturday and Sunday; a large number of people turned up, and a profit of one hundred and thirty pounds was made.

In November 1955 we celebrated Christopher's twenty-first birthday with a party for the tenants and our own people. We also gave a dance on New Year's Eve.

One night in bed, I counted up to find that the next summer would be the twenty-fifth Anniversary of the sailing of Gino's expedition for Greenland. Next morning, I looked up the date and found that it was July 6th. All the twelve surviving members of the Expedition served with Commissions in the last War. I wrote to them all and with one exception they said they would come and have dinner with me to mark the occasion. I then asked a few other people who had been a great help to the Expedition: the Captain of the *Quest* (Captain Schjelderup), Professor Debenham (of Scott's Expedition and a great friend of Gino's), the Bishop of Portsmouth (late Director of the Scott Polar Research Institute), Sir George Binney (the first of the present generation of Polar Explorers) and Stephen Courtauld (Chairman of the Committee of the Expedition). We had our dinner at "The Prospect of Whitby", the historic inn on the river, just below St. Katherine's Dock, from which the *Quest* had sailed twenty-five years before.

The dinner was a great success and we all enjoyed it. We drank the health of the Queen, the King of Denmark and the King of Norway, and a silent toast to the memory of Gino and Percy Lemon.

We brought our sledging flags, which were all hung up; the *Quest*'s flag, with its winged polar bear, was hoisted on the flagstaff over the river. I also brought the remains of the Union Jack which flew at the Ice Cap Station.

Here is the menu with translation from the Eskimo:

Salmon with smoke.	*Eqaluk puokmit.*	Smoked salmon.
Pemmican Soup.	*Creme Pemmicane.*	Thick soup.
Amassets.	*Angmagssalik Arpika.*	Grilled trout.
Fillet of seal.	*Faux-Filet de Phoque.*	Minute steak.
Bilberries with milk.	*Boubouka Imomit.*	Strawberries and cream.
Angry sledge dogs.	*Chien de Traineau Enragés.*	Devils on horseback.
Bad milk with Biscuits.	*Imok Aipok Iverkanemit.*	Cheese and biscuits.

For some time I have been interested in the Norse discovery of America. It is known from the Sagas that, after Eric the Red had discovered Greenland, his son Leif Ericson sailed to the West and discovered a land which he called Vinland the Good. This was about the year one thousand and three, some five hundred years before Columbus. The difficulty is to know exactly where Vinland was; we only know that salmon abounded and that wild grapes grew there. There are many theories about the position of Vinland. It has been located at various points of the long coastline between Labrador and Florida. Stones with runic inscriptions have been found in the middle of the United States. I intend, if I can, to take an expedition to Labrador to try to find any traces of the Vikings that may still remain.

A new Trust has just been started. It is called "The Augustine Courtauld Do-Good Fund". The Trust Deed provides that the Fund can be used for any purpose the trustees desire.

My daughter Perina is to be married in April of this year (1956). Her fiancé is Jeremy Fordham, a land agent in his father's firm, doing most of his work outdoors. They are to be married at St. Andrew's Church, Halstead, where I used to go with my father and mother and where Betty's wedding took place in 1931. The vicar there, the Reverend A. W. Swallow, was my chaplain when I was sheriff.

August Courtauld (left) as High Sheriff of Essex.

18

My Father

MY FATHER was a gentle, kindly man. His tall, spare figure, with its head of silver hair, was for many years a familiar sight in Essex as he walked to the factory or to see his friends. He was peaceable. Although he was old-fashioned, he never punished his children, and his two loves, outside his family, were the factory and his books.

His mother died when he was fourteen; Aunt Min then looked after the children until they were old enough not to need her. She then took up farming. Five girls in my grandfather's family survived. None of them married, except Aunt Cicely, who married her cousin. This was not surprising, since no man ever dared to come to the house, nor could the girls go out to see anybody; they were never allowed the carriage. But Aunt Min and Aunt Liz grew up to be remarkable women, and I think I should say something about them now.

Aunt Min was a farmer who hunted and shot. She wore short hair like a man and in the evening a sapphire blue velvet dinner jacket and a white lace jabot. Although she wore a skirt, there was, I believe, always a pair of breeches underneath it. She was inexpressibly kind, and, with her friend Mary Gladstone, always made us welcome to Knights at Colne Engaine in our youth. She was always interested in our doings: she herself had a yacht, *Petrona*, a yawl of about thirty tons. In this she used to sail about all over the place, and though it was uncomfortable in bad weather (*Petrona* being a bad sea boat), Aunt Min would never turn back and there used to be battles royal between her and her skipper, Griggs. She liked taking ladies with her and expected them to be as tough as herself. No powder was allowed on board, and everyone had to go over the side, with my Aunt, at seven a.m.

On one occasion, *Petrona* went aground in the Zuyder Zee in a gale of wind, with my mother-in-law and sister-in-law on board. The pilot burst into tears and Griggs said they must abandon ship. There was a tug standing by. This Aunt Min refused to do and there was a fearful row. It was always a great thrill in my schooldays when we got asked down to the boat to go trawling in the Blackwater. Poor Mary Gladstone, who looked after the commissariat, hated the whole thing. Apart from anything else, she was practically blind.

Aunt Min used to sell her apples from the farm to the shops in Frinton. One day she was highly delighted at being turned out of the ladies' room at Frinton Golf Club. The Secretary had spotted her top half through the window and had not seen her skirt.

For many years she was a member of Essex County Council, representing the Hedingham Division. Sometimes she and my Uncle Willie (later Sir W. J. Courtauld, Bart, who married my Aunt Cicely) found themselves voting on opposite sides. There were no party politics on the Council in those days. On one occasion, when Aunt Min was calling at houses asking people to vote at the coming election, she talked at length to a woman who came to the door, explaining what the County Council was and the importance of voting. The woman heard her out and then said: "I don't know what you're talking about no more than if you were my little cat."

Aunt Liz was the other remarkable Aunt. She was one of the first women in England to become a qualified Doctor. For many years she was a medical missionary in India—it was said she was once chased on her bicycle by a king cobra. In the War, she nursed in France and in the Great Serbian retreat; she was awarded the Croix de Guerre as well as a mention in despatches from Marshal Pétain (then a soldier) for "carrying on her nursing duties under continuous bombardment". She afterwards devoted her life to the village of Greenstead Green and Halstead Hospital.

There were also Aunts Ruth, Dorothy and Cicely. Aunt Dorothy liked slums and was always the soul of kindness. Aunt Cicely was a "cruelty fan"; she loved animals and was a great natural supporter of the RSPCA. The vermin in her woods had a very good time. Aunt Ruth is now ninety; she is lame and can no longer go out. In the last war, she thought it wicked to eat and used to put her food coupons on the fire. Aunt Ruth looked after my father until he married—but now to go back to him when he was still a boy.

At the age of sixteen he left Charterhouse to go into the family business, and lived with his father at Cut Hedge, Gosfield, riding his pony every morning to the Halstead factory. The working hours were then six a.m. to six p.m.

When my father entered the business, it was concerned with winding, dyeing and weaving real silk. Courtaulds were rather famous for their mourning crêpe, which was in great demand in Victorian times. In those days the firm was run by Sam Courtauld, my father's great-uncle. He was an autocrat. Only one member of the family in each generation was allowed to join the business. After Sam Courtauld came my grandfather, then my father.

About the beginning of the century, the firm began experimenting in the making of artificial silk, now called rayon. The business ceased to be a family concern in 1912; it became a limited company. The new invention achieved success in the twenties, and this brought my father great wealth. He did not "make" his money—it came to him, as it were, from the sky. He used to say that "the thing about having money is that you don't have to think about it."

My father went on living in the same quiet way. He did not go in for a grand house, a large yacht or the collection of treasures. "I'm like the cat," he would say, "I prefer my own fireside."

In spending his money, he liked bricks and mortar. Although he never built a house for himself (which he badly needed, since The Howe was a cold, poor place to live in), he built many for others. To begin with, he pulled down the old Halstead workhouse and built on the site twenty "Homes of Rest" for old people. They were to be allotted in the first place to those who had worked all their lives in the factory. Then he demolished a lot of slum cottages in Halstead and built in their place some fifty nice houses. These were inscribed with names from the books of his favourite author, Jane Austen. The first occupants of "Pride and Prejudice" did not like the name at all—they thought he was making fun of them.

He gave Bocking a fine village hall which stands near the factory where he used to spend so much of his time. To Bocking, too, he gave a playing field; it lies opposite the village hall. I remember going, as a boy, to the opening. He built another village hall at Blackmore End, where so much of his land was. This was designed for him by my father-in-law to be, Frank Montgomerie, and there we hold our Harvest Home. The Biochemistry Institute at the Middlesex Hospital was my father's gift at the suggestion of his old friend and fellow-member of the Board of the Middlesex, Sir Alfred Webb-Johnson, later Lord Webb-Johnson and President of the Royal College of Surgeons. He gave the Science Block to Felsted School, where he was Chairman of the Governors for twenty-six years. His chief interests in public work were the Standing Joint Committee (he was Chairman for twenty years), and the Royal Literary Fund. The first of these looks after the County Police; the second, writers fallen on bad times. He used to travel about the County a good deal in connection with Standing Joint Committee business, accompanied by the Chief Constable.

My father's tips were always modest—usually the sum of sixpence. I remember a great scene at Euston when the whole family, complete with baggage, was going off to Scotland. After the porter had finished loading the immense piles of luggage into the train, he advanced to my father for the tip. It was sixpence.

Most of my father's friends seemed to be doctors; he was lucky enough not to need them professionally. He liked to see how much they ate and drank, and to listen to their stories.

His love for his books was very real; he knew every volume in his library, and it contained many thousands. He could always point to any book you wanted, knowing exactly where to find it. Jane Austen's novels he knew word for word. His other favourite was Walter Scott, and he also had a great affection for Horace Walpole and Dickens. But the book that remained his greatest solace all his life was the Odes of Horace. He had learned his Latin under the great Dr. Page at Charterhouse. In 1908 he published his selection of metrical translations of the Odes and Epodes: here is an example—composed by my Grandfather:

"See! where Soracte's lofty brow
  Is mantled o'er with glistening snow;
How with the weight the forests bow,
  And clogged with ice the rivers flow!

"Pile, Thaliarchus, pile high up
  The blazing logs—keep out the cold;
Nor grudge, from Sabine jar, a cup:
  A brimming cup, of four-years-old!

"And to the gods leave all the rest
  The winds that fight the boisterous seas
Are silent at their high behest,
  Nor stir the ash or cypress trees.

"But how to-morrow's hours shall run,
  Or to what span thy years advance,
Ask not! Take all for good; nor shun
  The pleasant loves, and festive dance.

"Now, when remote is peevish age,
  And in the veins youth's ardour springs,
Prompt at the evening's tryst, engage
  In walks and tender whisperings.

"While from the nook the laughter tells
  Where hiding maid, in feigned alarm,
Feebly the sportive snatch repels
  Of token from her hand or arm."

                              George Courtauld

In later years he made revised editions of the book and in the course of preparing these had correspondence with many scholars and authors. His edition of Kipling had a personal letter from the author in every volume.

It should not be thought that my father was interested only in the classics. He read many modern books and used to write little notes in the margin. He told me once, having just finished Evelyn Waugh's *Decline and Fall*, "If I had ever written a book, that is the book I should like to have written."

In his quiet life nothing very exciting happened, but there were one or two pleasant things. I remember the dedication of a reredos which he gave to Bocking Church. Later in life, he used to make forays in Scotland for the grouse. For some years he had a small moor, Kindrochet, belonging to the Duke of Atholl. Once, when I was sixteen, the Duke asked me to go for a day's stalking in Atholl Forest. I found myself crawling behind his head stalker, Peter Stewart. Eventually I got a shot. It turned out to be a Royal.

My father liked entertaining his friends from Essex at Kindrochet. He most enjoyed sitting in the heather, or beside some gurgling stream, eating a good lunch. Although a fair shot himself, he never cared for grand shoots. He used to say, when the keeper had laid out the bag, "I don't want these birds. I wish I could bring them alive again."

Three men in succession served my father as chauffeur all his life. First, when I was a very small boy, there was Flood; he drove a very primitive De Dion Bouton. This was in the days before British cars were invented. After a few years, Howard took over. He remained with my father as both driver and loader until his retirement a year or two before my father's death. The third chauffeur was Saunders, who had been with my grandfather, as had the butler, Charles Plumb. Saunders had served in France as Haig's chauffeur and had had a leg blown off. When he came to my father, he had to drive with a wooden leg as well as look after the electric light plant at The Howe.

Charles, the butler, did not like London at all. He said the crowds were too much for him and that they used to knock the very pipe out of his mouth in the street. When some men broke into the dining-room one day and drank the port, Charles was most indignant.

My father had two amusements. One was fishing—the old-fashioned bent-pin system where you watch a little float which bobs. For hours he would sit by the pond, with a boy to put on the worms, trying to catch a perch. The other was his cat. The first Persian, Breeks, a wedding present, lived to the age of sixteen; then came Barts, another blue Persian. My father used to let the cat play on his desk or on the dinner table, much to the annoyance of my mother.

He knew about port, few men more. He paid not the least attention to what he wore; I have seen him go off to a big dinner wearing his morning-coat quite happily. Once he turned up at a function in Essex in his scarlet DL's uniform with plumed hat, and, on arrival, his braces burst. I also remember him leading a procession at the Felsted Speech Day dressed in his red LLD robes and a panama hat. He always changed for dinner, but usually wore his butler's made-up tie.

He had only one business, was the Director of only one company. He would walk from his house in Kensington to the City and, after lunch, home again. When the weather was not fit for walking, he used to go by tube. I have heard that at the Board he would confound his fellow Directors with awkward questions derived from the long-ago, and, sometimes, with Latin tags.

Two things he was very keen on. One was the family silver, made in the eighteenth century by his forebears who had been kicked out of France by the Roman Catholics, at the time of the Revocation of the Edict of Nantes, in 1685. My father had inherited some of it and from time to time he bought other pieces. When he retired from the Company after sixty-five years' service, the Board presented him with a fine tray made by Augustine Courtauld in 1722.

Some years before this, the Company decided to present gold watches to people who had done over thirty years service. I went to the first presentation by the Chairman—Sir John Hanbury-Williams—at Halstead Factory. Dear old weavers who hadn't been out of doors for years came along. Some of them had worked in the factory for forty and fifty years. My father had done the longest service and therefore came first.

His other passion was tidiness. There was never a scrap of paper on his desk, only the old, worn blotter, his pen, his old frog paper-weight and the inkpot. Every letter he got he either answered at once or pitched into the waste-paper basket. When he was making his collection of family letters, he said with great pride that he had been watching the stoker at the factory putting them in the furnace.

He couldn't bear fidgetting. He didn't like "bothers" either. Anyone, even a dog, getting to his feet in the room bothered him.

He was always much afraid of fire and used to spend quite a time raking out the logs before he turned in. His last words as he went to bed were always, "Be sure and put out all the lights." Latterly, my mother and father used to come and spend Christmas with us at Spencers. One day I went into our little library to see how he was getting on and found his chair and the panelling ablaze. My father was sitting happily behind *The Times*, and when I told him, he said, "What a nuisance!" and got up. He had a great dislike of draughts; all the windows were shut in spite of the large log fire. In addition he had put on the electric fire and pulled it so close to his chair that it had caused the blaze of which he was blissfully unconscious.

He took his turn as High Sheriff, following his father in 1916, and had some very interesting judges, Mr. Justice Avory and Mr. Justice Horridge among them.

During the last war, he became a Welfare Officer in the organization run by Sir Stuart Mallinson. Many soldiers were living in remote camps, out in fields, to man the search-lights. My father used to go round to these sites to see what the men needed. His uniform was an um band. He was seventy-five then, but used to enjoy talking to these soldiers stationed in lonely places and took particular pleasure in getting curtains for them from the factory.

He was eighty-seven when he died. I have a remarkable walking stick that survived him. For over forty years, I saw him use it but never thought of asking him what its inscription meant. It was carved for him by a friend, and the date on the handle is April 1909. On both sides is a Horace Sapphic, which runs as follows: *"Sapienter idem contrahes vento nimium secundo turgida vela rebus angustis animosus atque forte appare."* The best translation I can arrive at is this: "When conditions are good, don't carry too much sail; when things are bad, go flat out."

Six of us carried his body through the churchyard where so many of the family rest, and into the little church at Gosfield where he used to go as a boy. Bearing him there now were his butler, Kiely; his chauffeur, Peaple; his keeper, Holman; my brother-in-law, Ralph Rayner; my brother Peter and myself.

On his gravestone is carved one of his favourite lines from Horace,

"Integer vitae scelerisque purus."

which may be translated:

"He was an upright man of unstained heart."

Samuel Augustine Courtauld DL JP.

Afterword

I N T H E first edition of *Man the Ropes*, Courtauld included some of his poems, among which was this one written to his father:

Integer Vitae—S. A. C.

He, a man upright of heart unstained;
No strong defence, nor arms arrayed,
Nor sword, nor spear at hand,
No foe to fear, of evil unafraid.

Free is his heart from guile, free from fear,
Simple his joys, no man to harm;
Erect he walks afield,
No carking care is his, no wild alarm.

All vanity away, his friend a book;
The cat sits by the fire, content.
Logs on the hearth blaze high.
His thoughts are in the past; no deeds lament.

Easter 1956

August Courtauld didn't enjoy such a tranquil old age. He succumbed to multiple sclerosis in 1959, aged 54. His eldest son Christopher, who had already taken over responsibility for *Duet*, was with him when he died.

August and Christopher Courtauld in 1936.

August Courtauld

An Appreciation by his Children

August Courtauld on board Duet.

UGUST WAS a leader, throughout his life and he applied these qualities to fatherhood, the same as everything else he did. As a result, his children loved and respected him and desperately wanted his approval of what they did. He was very much the "Better drowned than duffers—if not duffers, won't drown" type of father. He assumed his children had the ability to succeed and by and large they did. On his boat *Duet* there were lifejackets, in a locker with all the oilies and sea boots, but I don't remember ever wearing one, nor were we ever shown how to put one on! For most of our childhood *Duet* was kept at Burnham-on-Crouch, where the tide runs strongly up and down the river. As a matter of course we were sent ashore in the dinghy for the shopping, regardless of conditions, and expected to bring the boat alongside without damaging the topsides. I don't remember ever receiving any training—we just did it! We children were seasick from time to time and he was sympathetic, but his remedy was derived from Captain Joshua Slocum, to drink sea water out of a bucket. This certainly made the condition no worse! I remember being at the helm one night going down channel, and he emerged from the companionway, picked up the canvas bucket, dipped it over the lee side, drank a long draught and disappeared down below to the chart table. Us boys had a much easier time than our sister Perina, who hated the boat. He was a man who was able to see the path ahead very clearly. He was able to plan with absolute certainty and once something was decided, he was very difficult to shift. His plans had very tight safety margins and, as a result, he quite frequently terrified friends who he sailed or drove with and risked his own life. When he was in Greenland, during Gino Watkins' 1931 expedition, he had decided that he did not want to abandon the whole object of keeping Meteorological records throughout the winter even after the appalling journey up to relieve the summer incumbents of the ice cap station. They had already consumed the winter food rations for two men, on the way up and abandonment was a very real possibility. Freddy Chapman, his leader for the relief party, used the strongest arguments, as did all his other companions, against remaining alone. But he had worked out that he would be fine, so he stayed.

I think my father assumed everyone had the same clarity of vision about challenges and risks that he had. This meant he glossed over many dangers and assumed everyone else would have the imagination to see them, which of course in many cases they didn't. In 1947 he took *Duet* to the West coast of Scotland. We children, with our Nannie, joined him in the school holidays. I remember on one occasion we had anchored off the west coast of Eigg. The children and Nannie were under the command of Perina and Chris then aged 14 and 13. Nannie could not swim and there were Julien aged 9, and Stephen 7 and another 9-year-old friend, eager to bathe on the fine sandy beach. When we reached the beach there was a considerable surf breaking on it which would have been realised by our father. By skilled boatmanship, Chris managed to land us without mishap. We all had a great swim, then the time came to row back to *Duet*, anchored about half a mile off. Getting the dinghy, through the surf, without broaching, was a difficult and dangerous task, but was managed superbly well by Perina and Chris. All, of course, without lifejackets. We were welcomed back aboard as though nothing had happened! My mother, meanwhile, stuck on board and helpless to do anything went through agonies of worry. This story would be treated by anyone hearing it today, with shock and horror! But to us, at the time, it was all just "the run of the mill".

We all feel greatly privileged to have had August as our father and benefitted from his unique ideas of up-bringing. The boys, of course, were able to enjoy the sailing, while Perina suffered greatly because of it. We only had him for such a short time. His Multiple Sclerosis started probably in the early 50s and he died in 1959. His MS took a cruel extra twist in altering his personality, such that he turned against those who he loved. Our mother during those years existed through a living hell. For this reason, she always thought that this book could have been so much better. The somewhat staccato style, in which he wrote it, is markedly different from his other writing— the short notes in his anthology of Arctic and Antarctic writings, From the Ends of the Earth, and the account he wrote of his time at the Ice Cap Station, in the official story of the British Arctic Air Route Expedition, Northern Lights. Even the youngest of his children, Susie, who was eight when he died and never knew him before he became ill, feels his life has a strong influence on her work as an artist.

Julien Courtauld

I REMEMBER MY father as an exceedingly busy man, who was usually late for lunch, because he had usually spent the morning serving on a committee connected with the County of Essex. Whether it was the County Council or the local lunatic asylum, he would give it his all. It is sadly ironic to write this as the terrible disease that attacked him so severely at the beginning of the fifties, paralysed him so badly that during his last years he was not able to move any part of his body.

He showed the same great courage then, as he had during the war, serving in the RNVR and more especially when he was buried under the Arctic snows. I think of his valiant entry in his diary: "I did not believe I was to leave my bones on the Ice Cap."

How awful never knowing if you would be found or not, his food and oil running out and with no one to share the frightful fears. And he was only 26.

Perina Braybrooke

A T SPENCERS, there was a Sunday morning Church inspection just inside the front door. We had to show clean shirts, washed hands, shoes polished, no marks on suits, ties tied before walking through the woods to church. We were then given sixpence for the collection while our father put in at least a pound note. There also were bedroom inspections to check properly made beds and a word of authority on never giving orders to any of the people he employed and always speaking to them with respect. I remember being asked to go and help Hardy, the determined hunchbacked handyman, wash the car and polish it properly and I remember Father listening with sympathy to Kiely, Grandfather Courtauld's butler, who had come to ask our father for help after he'd been arrested for attacking the cook at the Howe with a carving knife. However, I also remember him telling Betty to take this filth away and make some decent coffee and giving Eardley the butler the sack for refilling all the Gordon's Gin bottles with water. As Father never drank Gin, he hadn't discovered this until a friend had come over for a drink and asked for Gin.

I remember him pigeon shooting among the nettles and rabbit shooting at night from the open Bentley; tree felling in the park with the Danarm power saw or with his own axe. I remember his delight on driving the David Brown tractor along the drive and around the park. I remember him reading aloud by the library fire, either Dickens, or Somerset Maugham's Ashenden stories, or ghost stories, or on Sunday, the New Testament; playing chess, and occasionally allowing me to win. Once, after I'd been playing the piano, telling me he thought the piece I had been playing was the gramophone. I remember him being impressed by my hitching a lift from Windsor Station in the cab of a goods train when I thought I'd missed the school train.

I remember being told to go back and wash my hands more thoroughly before 1 p.m. lunch and mop the cloak room floor, being told at lunch to pick up the piece of food that had fallen on the floor and eat it, being allowed to stay up after dinner and asked why I didn't like the book of Revelation. I remember my amazement at his nonchalantly paying the bill for lunch at the Chequers Hotel in Newbury with a folded white five-pound note.

I remember him being furious when I invaded the heads on *Duet* while he was enthroned; telling me that drinking seawater was the only cure while I was being seasick with William into a canvas bucket.

I remember him typing out the individual duties for his four sons on board *Duet* (mine being cabin boy) and forgiving my letting the sail locker lid drop on my mother's fingers while she was at the helm, concentrating on winning a race and I will never forget him smoking his pipe with contentment and gazing up from the helm at the pennant flying above *Duet's* mains'l.

Stephen Courtauld

August, Perina, Christopher and Julien Courtauld at Spencers.

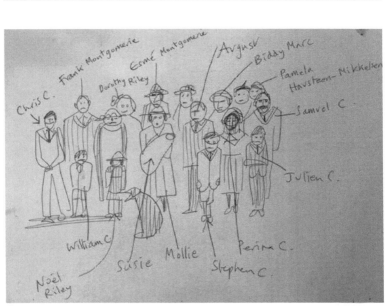

Susie's christening.

The Legacy of *Duet*

THE COURTAULDS have tended to think of *Duet* as a member of their family. She was most significant to August's oldest son, Christopher who had come aboard first in 1934, 'About which, he wrote later, "I remember nothing at all, being *in utero* at the time, though I am told we managed to fall overboard with my mother collapsing in laughter." After the war holidays on *Duet* became an important—and strenuous—part of family life and it was on one of these that Christopher fell seriously ill with polio, aged 13. He was lucky to recover. Though he suffered some degree of disability for the rest of his life it never stopped him sailing, though his wife, Elizabeth, recalls that very often he chose not to join shore parties, being content to remain alone with his beautiful yawl. She believes that *Duet* encapsulated the unusually deep love that Christopher had felt for his father.

Though Christopher probably didn't test Elizabeth in the same conscious way that August had tested Mollie when he invited her on holiday aboard Frank Carr's *Cariad* "to see how she would take to the sort of life I liked", it seems completely appropriate that he had asked her to marry him after she'd joined *Duet* for a sailing holiday on the west coast of Ireland. Christopher was then the hospital chaplain at the Royal London Hospital where Elizabeth was a young doctor.

"A week after returning I called on Christopher to thank him—said I would be brief as he was very busy in the hospital over the weekend. He said, 'Just one thing before you go—would you like to marry me?' I was stunned! I said 'I'll let you know'—and exited. Two days later I said yes and we had 35 years of happiness."

These years included many more holidays with *Duet* as a family boat but among Christopher's great achievements was the foundation of the Ocean Youth Club in order to give many other young people a taste of the sailing pleasure that meant so much to him. His daughter Sarah explains:

"For my dad, *Duet* provided him with a world of freedom and adventure. He sailed throughout his childhood, learning from August. After he had polio, Christopher couldn't run, ride or climb mountains. But sailing was a way for him to experience speed, agility and power in a way that he couldn't easily on land.

"Like August, he was a superb navigator and relished tricky passages. And though he had no aversion to sunshine, there was a particular gleam in his eye when he was at the helm with waves crashing over the side, or horizontal rain. He also inherited some of August's austere spirit, and loved getting everyone up at five thirty in the morning to catch the tide.

"Christopher did sometimes sail on modern, plastic boats as a concession to his family, but essentially thought of modern conveniences (such as winches) as cheating, and was much happier on board *Duet*. He was an incredibly calm skipper whatever the crisis of the moment might be—from a hat overboard to a rogue fishing boat crashing into us and ripping off the entire bowsprit.

"For my dad, sailing was a world away from the responsibilities of work, a world of camaraderie and merriment. I remember a crew member from one of his *Duet* trips reminiscing about bottles being divided into 'round' (wine) and 'square' (whiskey).

"He was a more relaxed and convivial character than his father, and sailed *Duet* in a less of a strict way, though like August he delighted in *Duet*'s racing spirit— happiest zipping along in light winds.

"Sailing meant so much to him, he wanted to share that pleasure with others—which is why he co-founded the Ocean Youth Club (now the Ocean Youth Trust) in 1960, with Chris Ellis, so that young people could enjoy sailing whatever their background. *Duet* was the flagship of the OYC for thirty three years, taking thousands of young people to sea. She took part in the Tall Ships Race many times, often taking home trophies (first overall in 1983 and 1994).

"In 1994 the OYC decided to switch to a modern fleet, and *Duet* found a home with other historic boats at the Cirdan Trust, still taking groups of young people to sea, on the East Coast. In 2012 she celebrated her centenary with a 2,000 mile voyage around the coast of the UK, with eleven legs, various seal and dolphin sightings, and considerable amounts of vomiting along the way. She is now the UK's longest serving sail training vessel, giving hundreds of young people adventures at sea every year, and is still used by the family for occasional holidays.

"So *Duet* now has a very different life from the one August first envisaged for her. At nearly 110 years old, she can't quite 'go anywhere', as August hoped, and she's had almost all of her parts replaced. But she still has all her elegance, grace and zip, and is very much alive."

Christopher Courtauld once wrote that one of the tributes to *Duet* that had pleased him most came from W. M. Nixon writing for *Yachting Monthly* about her participation in the 1975 Jubilee Fastnet Race: "She was a clear line honours winner in the gaff rigged section... She would also be a clear winner were there a competition for the yacht which has contributed most to sailing in this century. In her own quiet way, *Duet* has had an unrivalled career, and will thoroughly deserve all the honours which come her way this month at the OYC birthday party." Nixon's article was written in 1981, now, forty years later in 2021 (ninety years after the 26 year old August Courtauld spent his time under the Greenland icecap imagining her), *Duet* is owned by Christopher's daughter Sarah (a comedy writer, performer, and award-winning author of children's books), her husband Jonathan Weil and her cousin Toby (son of August's son William). She is managed by the Cirdan Trust.

Duet and the Cirdan Sailing Trust

Duet is now on permanent loan to the Cirdan Trust and has sailed with thousands of young people, many of whom experience some form of disadvantage in their lives. These include care leavers, those in the care of the local authority, those at risk of abuse, crime or exclusion, others from dysfunctional families or some who are just struggling in education. They come on board to live and work in a confined space at sea where they have to take part in all aspects of life on board, both above and below deck. They have to cook and care for themselves and each other and live in harmony with all on board. The experience helps them to build confidence, self-esteem, resilience and motivation, and develop life skills that can built upon back on dry land.

Duet still retains many of her original Edwardian features alongside the necessary safety and navigation equipment required to operate on a commercial level. She is operated by two professional crew and welcomes aboard groups of up to seven people for residential voyages—some of her bunks are very 'cosy'. Her compact galley is fully equipped with a small gas oven and hob, a small fridge and a sink and all the necessary utensils to live on board.

She tends to sail from the East and South Coasts with voyages of up to 7 days but in recent years has participated in the Tall Ships Races, is a regular competitor in the ASTO Small Ships Race, has sailed around the UK on several occasions and took part (probably for the last time) in the Fastnet Race in 2013. As well as taking groups of disadvantaged young people to sea, a limited number of voyages each year are set aside for students completing their Duke of Edinburgh gold award.

The Cirdan Sailing Trust was founded in 1983 by a local vicar, The Reverend Bill Broad, who used a substantial inheritance to set up the charity to provide personal development opportunities for inner city and disadvantaged young people. Cirdan presently carries out its work on a small fleet of three boats, one of which is *Duet*.

Having always been a generous supporter of Cirdan's work, prior to his death in 2014 Christopher Courtauld set up the 'Duet Fund', administered by the Essex Community Foundation. Each year funds are allocated to the maintenance and running of *Duet* alongside providing bursaries to subsidise individual voyage fees.

Whilst Christopher thought Cirdan's use of *Duet* for the disadvantaged was eminently worthwhile, he was keen to ensure young people from all walks of life have the opportunity to get on the water. During the school holidays, therefore, a limited number of voyages are set aside for students who are looking for a challenge to complete their Duke of Edinburgh Gold Residential Award, for which *Duet* is the ideal vessel.

There is no doubt that the COVID-19 pandemic has had a detrimental effect on some young people's mental health and, for others, has blocked the development of social skills and affected their confidence and motivation. The need for challenge, fun and adventure at sea has never been greater and thanks to Christopher Courtauld's legacy a great many young people will have memories to last a lifetime.

Leonie Back, Chief Executive of the Cirdan Sailing Trust

Quotes from Young People Sailing in 2021

"Being in the open air out at sea was so different to normal life, and while it was a challenge learning how to sail a boat, this was what made it engaging along with the spectacular scenery. Of course none of this could of been done without the support of the *Duet* Fund. It really was a life experience worth having. Like the staff and members at the Cirdan Sailing Trust, the supporters are the backbone of this Trust and are what preserve the magnificent heritage of the boats like *Duet* and the history that stands behind them. So thank you so very much for making it possible."

J. Andrews

"I would like to say a huge thank you for providing me with a brilliant opportunity that has made accomplishing my Gold Duke of Edinburgh residential such an extraordinary and special experience. I could never have anticipated bonding both so quickly and so effortlessly with all of my fellow crewmates on *Duet* that together created an incredible atmosphere of companionship throughout the voyage. I am hugely grateful for all of the new experiences and skills it has given me along the way from the very start, from the woven in responsibilities of being a crewmember, such as conducting night-watches, to rowing and gaining a new appreciation for sailing's fundamental technicalities. I sincerely hope that I will be able to come once again sometime in the near future!"

Matthew

"Then the fun started. Over the next few days, we were learning the ropes of *Duet*—by far the prettiest boat I have been on. Although a lot more physical than I had thought, I absolutely got the true experience of what it is like be a sailor. I loved every moment on *Duet*, but I'd have to say my favourite part was when we did our first anchor watch. I luckily managed to grab the 05:00-06:00 slot. We had anchored in this small bay surrounded by these picturesque cliffs."

Catherine Jane

"Every day was like an adventure, sailing around the Isle of Wight on a century old sailing boat was an experience I'll forever remember.

The time I spent on board *Duet* has made some of my favourite ever memories that I will hold for the rest of my life. Thank you so much for providing and funding this experience, I couldn't have had it without your support."

Archie

"The trip impacted my mental health in a remarkably positive way. It was an incredibly enjoyable experience that I would do over and over. I would particularly like to thank again the *Duet* Fund that enabled me to enjoy this fantastic experience."

Jacob

"Thank you so much to the *Duet* Fund for the generosity that has enabled me to spend a week on board *Duet* with The Cirdan Sailing Trust. I had the most amazing time and could clearly see a difference in my confidence and sailing ability throughout the week. The opportunity to spend time on *Duet* was even more special due to the length of time spent in lockdowns during the last year and half. The opportunity to meet new people and to spend time away from home was therefore even more beneficial. Also, throughout the lockdown I lost confidence in myself and during the voyage I was able to gain some confidence back."

Martha

The Cirdan Trust (Registered Charity No. 1091598) is based in Bradwell Marina, Waterside, Bradwell-on-Sea, Essex CM0 7RB

01621 776684 / info@cirdantrust.org / www.cirdantrust.org

Duet *today*.

Appendix

Passages of *Duet*

THE FOLLOWING passages of over two hundred miles have been made by the twenty-two ton auxiliary yawl *Duet* under my [August's] command:

Month Year	Trip	Sea Miles	Days	Average Daily Run Sea Miles	Weather
July 32	Burnham—Grangemouth	385	3.8	101	Fine weather.
Aug. 32	Oban—Penzance	413	3.5	118	East'ly gale down Irish Sea.
Aug. 32	Penzance—Burnham	337	3.4	99	Light airs.
June 33	Burnham—Heligoland	310	2.6	120	Light reaching winds. Race.
June 33	Nordeney—Burnham	278	1.7	164	Light fair winds.
May 34	Burnham—Heligoland	310	2.0	155	Light fair winds. Race.
May 34	Heligoland—Copenhagen	430	3.2	135	Strong wind from NW. Race.
June 34	Christiansand—Burnham	472	3.6	121	Light airs then strong fair winds.
June 36	Warsash—L'Aber-Wrac'h	205	2.0	102	Calm, light airs.
July 38	Burnham—Aberdeen	400	4.3	93	Variable and baffling winds.
Sept. 38	Inverness—Burnham	510	3.75	136	Light to strong West winds.

Month Year	Trip	Sea Miles	Days	Average Daily Run Sea Miles	Weather
June 39	Burnham—Bergen	575	5.8	99	Hove to in strong NW'r.
July 39	Stadt—Lerwick	228	1.7	137	Fresh fair winds and thick fog.
Aug. 39	Kirkwall—Burnham	523	3.9	134	Variable winds.
Aug. 47	Ymuiden—Aberdeen	366	4.0	91	Strong fair winds first night, then calms.
Sept. 47	Blyth—Burnham	278	2.8	99	Anchored off Lincolnshire coast for night.
Oct. 49	Teignmouth—Corunna	479	8.6	56	Headwind all the way.
Oct. 49	Corunna—Brixham	474	7.8	94	Full gale to hurricane from S to NW.
June 52	Dover—Maarstrand	564	4.3	151	Fair winds & light airs, for most of passage. Race.
June 52	Maarstrand—Copenhagen via Skaw	280	2.5	112	Fresh head wind then calm, strong beam wind to finish. Race.
July 52	Brunsbuttel—Burnham	368	2.3	156	Passage from Elbe under mizzen & headsails. Strong N'easter.
Aug. 53	Yarmouth—Grangemouth	304	2.7	113	Light fair winds.
Aug. 53	Inverness—Burnham	510	4.0	127	Strong wind off Yorkshire coast.
July 55	Fowey—Vigo Bay	545	4.1	120	Fresh N'easter all the way. Under squaresail.
Aug. 55	Cartegena—Palma	230	2.3	99	Calms, light airs and variable winds.

Index

Maritime Titles from Golden Duck

The Yachtsman Volunteers Collection:

- *The Cruise of Naromis: August in the Baltic 1939*
  G. A. Jones (with an introduction & afterword by Julia Jones)
- *Man the Ropes: the Autobiography of Augustine Courtauld—
  Explorer, Naval Officer, Yachtsman*
  Augustine Courtauld (with an introduction by Susie Hamilton)
- *From Pole to Pole: the Life of Quintin Riley* (forthcoming Spring 2022)
  Jonathon Riley
- *Maid Matelot: Adventures of a Wren Stoker in World War 2* (forthcoming 2022)
  Rozelle Raynes

The East Coast:

- *The Battle of the East Coast: 1939-1945* (forthcoming 2022)
  J. P. Foynes
- *The Deben* (biannual magazine)
  River Deben Association
- *Waldringfield: A Suffolk Village beside the River Deben*
  Waldringfield History Group

The Strong Winds Series:

1 *The Salt-Stained Book* (available as an audiobook)
2 *A Ravelled Flag*
3 *Ghosting Home*
4 *The Lion of Sole Bay*
5 *Black Waters*
6 *Pebble*
  Julia Jones (with illustrations by Claudia Myatt)

Books by Claudia Myatt:

- *Anglo-Saxon Inspirations: Designs to Colour and Create* (forthcoming 2021)
- *Keeping a Sketchbook Diary* (new edition forthcoming 2022)
- *One Line at a Time: Why Drawing Is Good for You and How to Do It*
- *Sketchbook Sailor*
  Claudia Myatt

We hold most titles in Claudia Myatt's RYA *Go Sailing!* series.

For a full list of Golden Duck titles, including the Allingham family series, *Wild Wood* by Jan Needle and the *Please Tell Me* activity books for older people, see golden-duck.co.uk. Most are additionally available as ebooks.